HOW TO GET OUT OF YOUR OWN WAY

SUNITA SEHMI

ARCHWAY
PUBLISHING

Archway Publishing books may be ordered through booksellers or by contacting:

Archway Publishing
1663 Liberty Drive
Bloomington, IN 47403
www.archwaypublishing.com
1 (888) 242-5904

ISBN: 978-1-4808-7643-9 (sc)
ISBN: 978-1-4808-7642-2 (e)

Library of Congress Control Number: 2019903957

Book Cover Design by Joanna Foray Mason

Print information available on the last page.

Archway Publishing rev. date: 05/20/2019

To my mother, Saroj Bala—Rani ("Queen" in Hindi) as she was so fondly called. She was unique, as all mothers are. And although our bond was complex, I learned that her kindness knew no limits, her generosity was immeasurable, and her insight was extraordinary. She is always in my heart, and her struggle and sacrifice will never be eclipsed from my mind.

Contents

STILL I RISE

You may write me down in history
With your bitter, twisted lies,
You may trod me in the very dirt
But still, like dust, I'll rise.
Does my sassiness upset you?
Why are you beset with gloom?
'Cause I walk like I've got oil wells
Pumping in my living room.
Just like moons and like suns,
With the certainty of tides,
Just like hopes springing high,
Still I'll rise.
Did you want to see me broken?
Bowed head and lowered eyes?
Shoulders falling down like teardrops.
Weakened by my soulful cries.
Does my haughtiness offend you?
Don't you take it awful hard
'Cause I laugh like I've got gold mines
Diggin' in my own back yard.
You may shoot me with your words,
You may cut me with your eyes,
You may kill me with your hatefulness,

But still, like air, I'll rise.
Does my sexiness upset you?
Does it come as a surprise
That I dance like I've got diamonds
At the meeting of my thighs?
Out of the huts of history's shame
I rise
Up from a past that's rooted in pain
I rise
I'm a black ocean, leaping and wide,
Welling and swelling I bear in the tide.
Leaving behind nights of terror and fear
I rise
Into a daybreak that's wondrously clear
I rise
Bringing the gifts that my ancestors gave,
I am the dream and the hope of the slave.
I rise
I rise
I rise.

Maya Angelou, 1928–2014, from *And Still I Rise*.

Foreword

Another world is not only possible, she is on her way.
On a quiet day, I can hear her breathing.

Arundhati Roy

How to Get Out of Your Own Way is about winning. If you believe you are born to win, then this book will help you plan, prepare, and act. When I was born sixty years ago, India was hardly ready to put its bet on women or to cheer girls to compete and win. I was fortunate, though, to have been born to parents who, like most traditional Indians, desired a son but were progressive enough not to shun or slight their four daughters. They raised us like sons and encouraged us to dream big. I was groomed by my father to go for the big kill—the highly coveted but formidably elusive Indian Administrative Service (IAS). He understood how tough this challenge was—thousands of the brightest of the bright competed, over and over again, for fewer than one hundred slots each year—yet he deeply believed in me and my ability to succeed. I am glad I could prove him right by acing the IAS at the incredibly young age of twenty-two.

This marked the beginning of my leadership journey in a male-dominated world. I was catapulted into an orbit that was veritably daunting, replete with complex strategic, management, and execution challenges—rogue politicians, unscrupulous and ruthless power lobbies, poverty, multitudinous deprivation of people, endemic underdevelopment, gross gender disparities, catastrophic calamities such as floods, fires, and communal riots, and a chronic scarcity of resources. At the same time, there were infinite opportunities to learn and develop, be creative, usher in transformative change, and make a profound difference in the lives of millions of people—their education, health, livelihoods, physical safety, and social security. As you would expect, this journey was not devoid of conundrums and taught me the abiding value of fearlessness, courage of conviction, and tenacity. I was able to break the proverbial glass ceiling by succeeding in roles and assignments that, in the past, had been the exclusive preserve of men. As I glided from the provincial to the national to the international arena, my canvass continued to expand and become more variegated. My faith proved bigger than my fears and gave me the strength to make *impact* the guiding mission of my life.

Sunita Sehmi, the author of this book, the female protagonists in her case studies, and I have much in common. We all faced vulnerabilities but refused to be held back and surged ahead. Our stories are real; the lessons are invaluable. Success requires a winning mindset, self-awareness, and adaptation. If any one of the variables in this equation is weak or missing, you are bound to feel impeded. Executive coaching can be of immense value in bolstering your self-confidence and bringing greater clarity about yourself, your needs, your goals, your emotions, your beliefs, your insecurities, and your blind spots. This paves the way for self-reflection, adaptation, and change. In today's world of soaring ambition and fierce competition, coaching can quietly unlock one's innate potential to excel.

How to Get Out of Your Own Way is a book that coaches you in a manner rarely attempted before. It is a distillation of insightful concepts enriched by Sunita's own very authentic personal and professional experiences. The author's unabashed account of her own predicament, interspersed with travails of her numerous clients, make the book highly compelling. There is simple but profound guidance that will resonate strongly with all those who are on a development, management, or leadership voyage. For instance, empathy and putting yourself in another person's shoes is vital. Building self-awareness is not a one-time act but a lifelong effort. Humble process enquiry is the critical first step towards establishing trust. Promoting a culture of giving and receiving constructive feedback is an imperative. Readers are reminded that these fundamental skills need deliberate and consistent investment, as they do not come easy and may be completely lacking in many cases.

It is refreshing that women are at the centre of this book. In the course of my work, I have witnessed a spectrum of gender inequality—from severe oppression and crass discrimination to subtle denial of equal opportunities. It is not common knowledge that nature has endowed women with a biological advantage over men, but this advantage is nullified by adverse social and economic circumstances that women often face. It is thus not unusual for even the most gifted of women to suffer from self-doubt or low self-worth. Fighting deeply entrenched stereotypes about gendered roles can be tough on women, leading to behaviours that may limit their personal and professional growth or jeopardize their work-life balance. This book is a call to women to aspire unhesitatingly, self-actualize boldly, and pursue happiness without guilt. Women have to be women's best friends and coaches as they are very familiar with each other's pain and difficulties.

I am glad Sunita rose to be that friend, guide, and coach to those numerous women who are talented, have dreams, and can realize them by freeing themselves of their self-imposed shackles.

Anuradha Gupta, Deputy CEO at GAVI, the
Vaccine Alliance

It is better to conquer yourself than to win a thousand battles. Then the victory is yours. It cannot be taken from you, not by angels or by demons, heaven or hell.
Buddha

About Anuradha Gupta

Anuradha Gupta is a global development leader with a track record of transformational impact at both the national and global level. She is passionate about women, adolescents, and children, in particular their health and education.

Currently deputy CEO of Gavi, the Vaccine Alliance, an international organization bringing together public and private sectors with the shared goal of creating equal access to new and underused vaccines for children living in the world's poorest countries, Anuradha oversees Gavi's strategy, policy, and programs across seventy-three countries.

PREFACE

> Women, as the minority, have to prove their worth all the time. We tend to over-prepare, over-study, over anticipate, we tend to overdo it.
>
> Christine Lagarde

When my clients ask me, "Is it really possible to change?" I always tell them the same thing: "If I can, you can; there is nothing extraordinary about me." And still, to this very day, I am continuously amazed and deeply touched by the ways in which people make profound transformational changes that impact their lives and the lives of others. They often thank me, and I remind them that it is they who shaped this change, not me. I am only here to ask questions and to enable them to become the leaders of their own lives. Indeed, the world out there is our projection, and we perceive the world how we would like to see it. It is only when I started asking myself questions that my own transformation started to happen, because if we want to really find our truth, we have to examine ourselves first. And what I know for certain is that once you become the master of your own self, no one and no circumstance can reduce you. It is your responsibility to assume accountability.

I see coaching as a profession that helps individuals and groups improve their performance on an emotional level. Our role as coaches is to help our clients work through issues that may inhibit them from being successful. Coaching is not merely positive thinking. Many sessions include examining personal information that clients have. The idea is for the client to realize his or her own solutions, strategies, and schemes. Good coaches build relationships swiftly. This involves the exceptional ability to understand people's needs, strengths, and weaknesses.

I am transparent with my clients. I am compassionate and challenging. I do not allow people to change my opinion of someone or a situation. I always remain objective and hold the mirror up to my client with the intention of further growth. I believe this is what makes me trustworthy and why my clients believe in me. In my humble opinion, trust is a key to coaching. Coaching can help identify what the client really wants out of her professional life, helps her appreciate the skills and experience he has amassed, and helps her identify opportunities and a network of contacts.

I am passionate about coaching and have always loved supporting people. Coaching was a very natural career choice. It was like following my personal destiny. I set up Walk the Talk with the intention of ensuring that people feel fully heard and seen. I aim to help people get out of their own way, to help them obtain a winning mindset. Winning can mean different things to different people. Therefore, my role is to be a supporter and a guide. I work with clients on topics like diversity management, effective collaboration, inclusion, leadership, and emotional intelligence (their EQ). I serve both private and government organizations and executive institutions, locally, globally, and remotely.

In today's world, both on a personal and professional level, we are certainly facing intense pressure like never before. There are so many challenges and constant changes in life that require us to be equipped to adjust and adapt, both incessantly and instantaneously. And this book is not meant to provide quick fix; I don't believe in quick fixes, as they rarely work in the long term. Rather, I would like you to use *How to Get Out of Your Own Way* as a guide, a manual for you to dip into and out of when and if you should need to. You will choose when you need it, and you will determine your progress. You will decide how much effort you will invest and how serious you are about your purpose. We are all unique, so you will need to shape my recommendations to work for you.

This book offers an opportunity for you to dig deeper, to be curious about yourself and others. It is simply a road map to help you along your way in your life and all that it brings, including the anxiety that surrounds personal change and growth. What I can tell you is that you cannot be there for other people unless you are there for yourself, and the paradox of knowing yourself is that you understand others better. Consequently, the biggest success for me will be if this book provides you with a space to self-reflect and explore and if, as a consequence, this deeper appreciation of yourself has a ripple effect on those around you and beyond.

My wish is that this book will help you to have an enriched, deepened, and expanded vision for the most important subject in your life: you. Through the use of challenging enquiries and personal stories, this book will provide support and help you to get out of your own way for good! If you are looking to become more resilient, build your self-confidence, and release the upsets and anxieties that are holding you back, this is book for you. Whoever you are and wherever you are from, this book is for everyone.

I think the most dangerous thing we can say to ourselves is "I have always been that way" or "I am too old to change." These are auto discounts, self-traps that keep us stuck, wedged in the past. The way forward requires effort to implement, and the fundamental obstacle is our archaic reasoning. Hence, my profound wish is that you meet yourself in this book and come to some acknowledgement and acceptance of yourself.

I have used theories and practices from executive coaching, developmental psychology, spirituality, religion, and neurolinguistic programming to help readers go from learning to application.

This book can help you develop a deeper sense of self-awareness and compassion for yourself and others. Although psychology has informed us for years, we still tend to underestimate the interplay between mind and body. How we are feeling physically affects the quality of our thinking, and we know from neuroscience that our emotional state affects chemicals and hormones in our body. Keeping our minds open at every age and stage in our lives, being curious, and being adaptable are the keys for a contented life. Yes, this book cheers you on to become a member of the "Lifelong Curiosity Club", where the membership is free and freeing. It encourages you to build a progressive mindset. Members of this club learn more than they instil, contribute more than they acquire. They do this with humility, acceptance, and compassion, and you can too. So, surrender and allow yourself this time. Give yourself permission to meet yourself, step back, and get perspective on the most valuable topic in your life: you! We can all be great. Yes, it's your time to step up and shine!

I am not here to be directive. I wrote this book simply because I wanted to share what worked—because I believe this is a practice which was successful for my clients and me, and now we I hope you can benefit. I am living my truth, and now I help others get out of their own way. In my work and in my life, I encourage people to acknowledge that it is often our very selves, not others, who inhibit our growth. In my experience, I see that most problems persist because of unobserved or unnoticed influences that keep us stuck. I am always learning new things about myself and other people. Consequently, as I understand, I impart with the intention to help others grow.

I have learned how my early experiences as a child and as a young adult have affected who I am today. I started to notice how some of my patterns of behaviour trickled into many of my relationships and how I have consciously or unconsciously learned to handle myself and others. This has enabled me to understand more about myself and has allowed me to make changes in my life.

This overwhelming feeling that I exist, that I am worth it, was partly the result of considered practice. It is a concept established by Anders Ericsson, Swedish psychologist and professor of psychology at Florida State University. Ericsson studies skilled performance in fields such as medicine, music, and sports, concentrating solely on extensive deliberate practice as a means of how proficient players attain their high-class performance.

Deliberate practice indicates a distinctive kind of repetition that is determined and regular. Certainly, consistency helped me to sustain the drive I created. Deliberate practice is a specialized and particularly effective form of purposeful practice. An experienced teacher or coach designs the training exercises and monitors a student's progress, modifying the training as necessary to keep the student progressing steadily. Anyone can apply these same methods on the job. This kind of deliberate practice can be adapted to anything—life, love, and letting go of unhelpful patterns.

The crucial element is an awareness of what it takes to become an expert and, therefore, becoming better equipped to maintain the deliberate practice essential to construct new skills. I believe and am living proof that there is no good evidence so far that proves that genetic factors related to intelligence or other brain attributes matter when it comes to less physically driven pursuits. In Anders's words, it requires dedicated devotion, guided with the specific goal of improving performance.

For me, the crucial element was a deep self-awareness and an awareness of what it took to construct new skills. Hence, I was consistent and persistent and used trusted advisors to give me feedback. I made sure I surrounded myself with people who encouraged me. I actively sought individuals from whom I knew I could learn helpful habits, whether these were professors, friends, family members, or clients.

It was not enough to have the knowledge and understanding, even though I had it on an intellectual level. I had to go through the painful process and *do the work* with dedication and diligence, facing it head-on. I am a real believer in deliberate practice. Consequently, when any new clients come to me, I always provide "homework" prior to their coaching and during our sessions. This helps them think through what they want to focus on and what they want to achieve. The consistency and real-time feedback is a form of deliberate practice.

For me, through daily exercise, I became more aware of my behaviour and stopped functioning like a walking emotional victim and stopped inviting disrespect from others. Slowly but surely, I learned that life is OK, and I saw that, for the most part, I was inhibiting myself from a life of worth and fulfilment.

Thus, I gained control over the situation to avoid massive destruction. By no means is deliberate practice a relaxing endeavour; it requires persistent determination and deliberation. Those of us who manage to master deliberate practice are dedicated lifelong learners, forever examining and investigating.

Through this practice I stopped complaining and blaming. I took control and I got my power back! Practice doesn't make perfect, but deliberate practice does.

When I started to understand and take responsibility for the way I was, I also realized how I have internalized the experiences I had as a child which have influenced me as an adult. I am now more accepting of myself and how I feel. I am "good enough" the way I am. I hope that you feel this too.

We are so preoccupied that we don't realize what we are feeling most of the time or the emotion behind our state. On the other hand, when we learn to understand and identify our feelings, we are better able to focus and therefore have better outcomes.

One of the most elusive things in life is true happiness and contentment, and knowing ourselves takes us a step towards achieving this. Once we understand our behaviours, we can change them. However, if we don't recognize them or acknowledge them, we will remain stuck, and our struggles will linger. This applies to you and to me. It is part of the human condition. I know for sure that my purpose is to repair, help, and by osmosis perhaps heal myself. That's OK; I own it, and my passion is promoting others.

I have come to realize that the women who need coaching the most are the ones who don't have enough money to pay for it, and thus coaching has become a luxury available to those who are affluent. Hence, I have dedicated this book, and myself, to supporting, guiding, and helping all in order to bring real change. Throughout my life, helping and supporting people has been my raison d'être, my purpose both personally and professionally. I am not an expert; rather, I like to think of myself as a guide on this journey of examination because I have visited this sphere many times before. I have been on many journeys, as we all have, and we can only tell our own stories. And this is my story, my reality. My hope for a better past nearly spoiled my present and my future until I got out of my own way.

Structure of the Book

Every chapter is titled with an homage to one of the popular hits of the 1980s. This is for two reasons. First, music has played a huge role in my life, and to this day I use music to lift me, to compose myself, and to celebrate. Second, I am unapologetically an '80s girl. This was an exciting and magical period for me, when I went on my path of personal discovery and intense innovation. I like to think of these songs in their original formats. No cover stories. I have done enough of them in my life.

At the end of each chapter, there is a piece called "Coaching Story". Here I share what I have learned during my meetings. These are stories about things that I have observed while coaching people. These are a few of many personal stories that have touched me. All names have been changed for confidentiality purposes. You will see from the stories that I do not position myself as the expert or the authority. We are all in this together on this human journey, and no person is immune to the tragedies of existence. No one is better. No one is wiser.

I am merely asking questions, not fixing, not mending, just being present and enquiring. I hope that you enjoy these journeys and can relate to them. They depict great strength, courage, and compassion. And one the most important things to remember is that the stories are about real people, from real people, in real situations. I have so much admiration for them because all of them did the *work*. They were not looking for quick fixes, tactics, or schemes; they understood from the get-go that this is hard work. It necessitates reflection, soul-searching, and some very tough exchanges. I am forever very grateful that these people understood this.

Each chapter also has a short personal story and applicable content; thereafter, there is a subheading, "How to Get Out of Your Own Way". A specific subject is appropriated to each chapter. There is also a coaching part, where you will be asked questions and given information and guidelines. I will be there every step of the way if things get tough.

My responsibility is to hold the space between us, carry the light on your path, and help you identify gaps. I will act as ally, making sure you focus attention on what is working and what is not. Your responsibility is to drive the process. You will decide how and when. I will be here in the passenger seat with the tools you need to realize your wishes and dreams.

One of the principal conjecturers of attainment is self-awareness. This is your time to develop a deeper self-awareness, press the pause button, and use this space to untangle feelings and desires. My approach is not a cookie-cutter one, not one-size-fits-all. What I want for you is to be better, live better. My mission is to bring coaching into people's lives, and not just for the elite few. I want to make coaching accessible to everyone, whoever you are, whatever you do, and wherever you live.

Like with anything, practice is essential, which is why I encourage you to journal and take notes. The more conscious you become of yourself and your actions, the more skilled you will become at getting out of your own way.

Summary

Ready to change the rest of your life? Great! Let's begin.

How to Get Out of Your Own Way

Mere repetition of an activity won't lead to improved performance. Your practice must be intentional, repetitious aimed at improving performance and combined with immediate feedback from a coach.

Professor Anders Ericsson, the expert on experts

1. Get energetic.
2. Fix precise and credible objectives.
3. Escape from your comfort zone.
4. Remain regular and determined.
5. Get feedback.
6. Take time out to recuperate.

Go to the journaling section on page 128.

Note any thoughts and opinions.

In what manner are you getting in your own way?

Coaching Story: Emma

I was once coaching a client who was advised by her line manager to receive coaching to help her with delegation skills. Like most coaching missions, this one presented with more than one issue. It is our job as coaches, together with the client, to disentangle the mess to find out what the real issues are. While I was coaching this particular client, her mother died. I knew from her story that although her mother was eighty-five and had lived a good life, the loss my client felt was profound. My client had lost her father when she was age seventeen, and her mother had single-handedly brought up her and her sister. My client's mother never remarried, never grumbled, and always did her best for her daughters. When my client's mother died, it took a heavy toll, and my client was deeply unhappy.

Our mid coaching meeting with my client, her sponsor, and me was planned a few weeks after her mother's funeral. During this meeting, I was taken aback by the "business as usual" attitude of the sponsor. I felt uneasy and uncomfortable discussing my client's coaching outcomes and not addressing the recent death of her mother. I saw this as an integral part of who she was. The impact on her and her work surely had to be addressed, didn't it? At one point in the discussion, when my client was being asked to make more progress, the conversation advanced, and her coaching sponsor asked about whether there had been any real change in her behaviour. He went on to outline what changes he would still like to see. I looked at my client. She was nodding, but she was not present. I took a risk. I turned to her sponsor and said, "Could I ask a question?"

"Yes, sure," said the sponsor.

"Were you aware her mother passed away a few weeks ago?"

"Yes," replied the sponsor, "but I don't think it is appropriate to bring it up now. I think it is too personal to talk about."

I turned to my client. "Would you like to talk about it?" I asked her.

"Yes," she answered. "Yes, I would."

There was silence. Then her sponsor asked those wonderful three words: "How are you?"

"It has been hard to concentrate since I got back from the funeral. I didn't want to make a fuss, but I am finding it really hard to focus. Thank you for asking me. I wanted someone to ask how I was, how I *really* was doing."

Those three words changed the course of the conversation, their working relationship, and the coaching. Coaching provides a safe space to understand. A coaching relationship is a place where you can show yourself and can continue the conversation even when there might be discomfort or fear. It is a relationship with boundaries, a laboratory for testing out ways of operating in the world. We are all layered and sometimes conflicted as individuals. As coaches, we are on the same team as you.

My client was emotional and happy to share. She and her sponsor spent the rest of the time talking about shared loss and the impact, and I and my client's sponsor discussed how we could both support her. Empathy is showing genuine concern about the *person*, not just their performance. If your friend or a loved one lost her mother, would you show care? Of course you would. So why should it be different at work? It is not rocket science; it's compassion in action. I have seen in my life that when disaster happens, I come to see the genuine side of people, those who step up and support and those who cannot step up and support for whatever reason. My learning is that nothing is evident, so check things out before making assumptions. Like a great client once told me, to *assume* makes an *ass* of *u* and *me*!

CHAPTER 1
Forest Fire

> I learned compassion from being discriminated against. Everything bad that's ever happened to me has taught me compassion.
>
> Ellen DeGeneres

I was born in London in the sixties. My parents were Punjabi immigrants who left India for the United Kingdom, hoping for a better life and better days ahead. My parents lived in extremely difficult circumstances as children, and they didn't have much money at all. Hence, having seen the partition in India, they were consumed by the ghosts of division, the struggle for economic survival. They moved to London in the 1950s, where both economic and financial stability were assured—at a price. The Indian community that moved to London in the fifties had seen both violence and viciousness during the partition. The stories were universal and stayed with them, flashing in their dreams, often unspoken as the grief was overbearing. My parents worked hard, and like most immigrant stories, their life was a daily struggle. I recall my parents wanted us children to "fit in", but essentially they wanted us to be Indian, specifically Hindu. I grew up in a context where I was constantly reminded that we were Indian, we were immigrants, and we were different. I got this message incessantly inside and outside my home.

From an early age, I noticed that everyone around me talked about "difference" in a very decisive way. I was often reminded that outside was not safe, as there are two types of people—"them" (the whites) and "us".

"Be very careful. They are not like us," my father would say.

"How are they different?" I would ask.

Then, with true seriousness and conviction, my father would say in his thick Indian accent, "Vell, did you see the shelves in the supermarket? They only eat tinned food."

At school, more abstract and absurd comments were made by my friends.

"Yuck, what's that smell?"

"Soap," I would answer innocently.

"You smell of curry. Do you eat curry for breakfast?" they would retort.

"No, l am just like you. I eat cornflakes."

Just like you ... I am just like you—so desperate was my need to assimilate.

Indeed, the 1970s in Britain was a critical and challenging time for Indians and other minorities, as well as for the indigenous population. Britain's workforce scarcities had created a massive post-war migration from India and Pakistan. The open-door immigration policy with Britain's former colonies was to reinvigorate the economy.

Trying to find a home for these people and their families in 1950s Britain was punitive, and most were met with discrimination and hostility. My mother told me that when she arrived in London, as she and my father looked for a room to rent, they were met with a cautionary message positioned on the door: "No blacks. No Irish. No dogs." The message was clear: we were not welcome. And when you are in a different country that does not really value the country you are from, it's always a battle to clutch onto who you are.

On top of that, few immigrants were able to get a job which corresponded to their credentials. As a result, my father was in a perpetual state of resentfulness and fury. He held an English honours degree and had taught in Kenya. However, when he arrived in England in the 1950s, he could only get a job in a factory, as his diplomas were not recognized. My mother told me that when she'd arrived in London at the tender age of seventeen, the only job she could get was washing clothes in a laundromat. She would weep years later at the shame of washing people's clothes, a job that in her hometown she would never have been expected to do.

Most of the initial newcomers to Britain in the 1950s and 1960s tended to settle for jobs beneath their capability and their ability. For their generation, the sacrifices would be worth it as long as their children studied and succeeded. But there was a price they paid—we all paid—living in rage, resentment, and vehemence. Even when their financial circumstances improved, for some the bitterness did not.

My parents and their community had no idea what was about to hit them. I cannot imagine what it must have been like to deal with that kind of animosity and the sense of not belonging. It's painful when you feel like you don't belong or when you're treated like the outsider. There was unease for all involved. Like most mass immigration stories, there was a stream of anxiety on both sides. Nobody was prepared.

The most difficult challenge I had to overcome as a child was being the second girl in a family where the pressure to give birth to sons rather than daughters was tremendous. My mother would often tell me that when she was in the hospital for my birth, she was so disappointed after finding out she'd had another girl that she did not pick me up for two days. I remember my mother repeating this story when I was a little girl and well into my adulthood.

"I could not even look at you when you were born. I was so disappointed. I felt like a failure. Can you imagine?" She added in all seriousness, "All my friends had boys except me! I was the only unlucky one who had a girl!"

The manner in which she recounted this story pierced my heart every time she told it. Frequently, she divulged the fact that the nurse at the hospital forced her to pick me up, as she didn't want to touch me. I was an unwanted girl child, and my mother struggled to come to terms that she had yet another daughter.

It became a source of entertainment in the family that she did not want to pick me up, as she was she sure that the hospital had swapped the babies and given her boy to someone else. I was a *firangi* (meaning a foreigner). I imagine for my mother, having a boy would have meant that she was a real woman, adding value and respect to her husband's family. Having another girl was a punishment.

What I know to be true is that the impact of not feeling wanted or safe showed up in my behaviour years later. Whenever psychological safety was absent, I was in a state of internal panic. Certainly, it was very tough to live in an atmosphere where I was repeatedly reminded that I was just a mistake and not supposed to be here. Until I became aware of the impact of my old injuries, I would get triggered by them and make any sense of conflict between people about me, when it was not about me.

Any situation that would remind me of a previous context where I had felt hostility or danger would trigger the alarm bells to go off. So, I suppose the gender odds were against me the day I was born. Convinced that I was going to be a boy, my mother had even chosen a name, Sunil, but sadly for her, Sunil became Sunita—and that is where my struggle began.

The messages I got were hard and relentless:

> "Just study enough so you get a good husband."
> "Don't shine too much that you make the boys look unimportant."
> "Behave like a girl" (whatever that means).

These "innocuous" comments were subtle but relentless, hailing from my parents, aunties and uncles, communities, and neighbours.

For some reason, nobody showed much discretion when it came to gender prejudice.

In 1968, two years after I was born, Enoch Powell made his infamous "Rivers of Blood" speech. Powell spoke about excessive immigration and expressed his sentiment that the influx of immigrants was "getting out of hand".

Now nearly fifty years later, the animosity Powell spoke about is being kept alive by hate speeches delivered by politicians in countries across Europe and the USA.[1]

Powell's speech exacerbated the feeling of exclusion my parents and other immigrant families felt in Britain. Never welcome, not wanted, we received the fundamental message that we were excluded. For me, there was a constant desire to be an insider while knowing I did not fully fit in. I felt continuously tangled, internally knowing that I "ought to" have the same apprehension and worries about the "whites" that my parents had but that I did not have. I don't really understand why, but I repetitively looked beyond colour, and very early on I saw that while everybody was talking about difference, I could see that we all had many similarities.

My parents' generation who came to the UK in the 1950s and 1960s had adopted an attitude of turning the other cheek when faced with discrimination. My mother would say, "When you are on the outside, your only goal is wanting to be on the inside." Except that we, the second generation of Indians, regarded ourselves as insiders. We were British citizens almost immediately.

Great was my own need to integrate. At primary school when I was the age of seven, during our weekly circle time, Mrs Booth, my class teacher, would ask us one by one what we'd had for lunch over the weekend. It was a question I dreaded as I remember listening to my English friends naming typical British foods like roast beef, mashed

---

[1] For the full text of the "Rivers of Blood" speech, see Appendix A.

potatoes, trifle, bread, and butter pudding. I feared this question every week, and every week I lied.

There was no way I was going to say we had roti,[2] dahl, and turnip *subji*. So, I fibbed every week, and I had a feeling Mrs Booth caught on to my deceit, as my typical English meals got more extravagant and more excessive every week. Essentially, I lived two lives, had two identities, and had two ways of being. At school, I would talk about *Top of the Pops*, and at home, I would watch Hindi films. Bollywood was our access to India. Masala movies,[3] love stories, and family dramas kept us hooked, and we felt a part of India even though we were not physically there.

The complications of growing up struggling with being British and trying to live up to my parents' Asian cultural traditions was troublesome and tiresome. As a British Indian, I believe my experience reflects the balancing act between the culture I was born in and the culture I was raised in. What is more, nobody is ever just one thing. Thus, these feelings of confusion and conflict around what could and couldn't be said, in fear of being judged, affected my confidence about being different. I feared being rejected because of my difference. Therefore, I felt I was I constantly wearing a mask, swapping it effortlessly, so it would seem, between home and outside life. My life was a mélange of *Grange Hill*[4] and the gayartri mantra.[5]

It was a "persona" as Carl Jung described, a guise, a pretext, the

[2] Roti is flat round bread cooked on a griddle. Dahl is a heavy Indian stew made from lentils. Subji is a dish consisting of vegetables cooked in gravy.
[3] Masala movies are a mix of action, comedy, romance, music, and drama. They are named masala because this is a mixture of spices in Indian cuisine.
[4] *Grange Hill* was a British children's drama series produced by the BBC in 1978.
[5] The gayartri mantra is a highly revered mantra from the Rig Veda dedicated to Savitr, the sun deity. Gāyatrī is the name of the Vedic metre in which the verse is composed. The mantra's recitation is traditionally preceded by om and the formula "bhūr bhuvaḥ svaḥ", known as the *mahāvyāhṛti*, or "great (mystical) utterance".

thing that one presents to the world. This was the survival mechanism I intuitively picked up, because growing up in London at that time for me was pure torture. There was always a comment, an incident, an event reported on the news or witnessed, all emphasizing that we were outsiders, not wanted, and not welcome—and I hated it. I remember senseless statements like, "I hate blacks, but you're all right" and "Listen, I got nothing against you. It's the rest of the Pakis I can't stand."

I particularly remember an incident when I was thirteen. I had a really good school friend named Greg. He had white-blond hair and a soft, pale complexion. Greg and I could talk for hours about life and school, and although we had very different backgrounds, we had a good friendship, or so I thought. One Monday morning, Greg walked into our math lesson, and as he entered the room, my jaw dropped. His razor-cut scalp, tight jeans, black boots, and Union Jack scarf around his neck had all the signs that he had become a skinhead. At that point in time in the UK, the word *skinhead* had become synonymous with neo-Nazism, fascism, and racism.

Greg walked into class and looked straight ahead. He gave me no eye contact, no smile, no hello. He walked up to his desk behind mine but did not acknowledge me. I felt very confused and dejected. I just could not understand what had happened. Why was he so distant?

Class started, and the teacher began explaining complicated fractions and writing on the blackboard, but I could not concentrate. And I also could not help myself. I turned around to talk to Greg, who was sitting behind me.

"Hi, Greg. What's going on? You OK?"

I remember Greg looking at me. He was cold and angry, and I will never forget what he said as he looked straight into my eyes.

"Fuck off back to your country, Paki."

I was stunned, immobilized by his insult. *You as well?* I thought. If it was his intention to wound me, then he had succeeded.

At that point, the math teacher noticed I had my back to him and shouted, "Sunita, will you stop talking and turn around? I don't know how many times I have to tell you!"

I did not hear the rest. Fighting back the tears, I just snapped and retorted, "Sorry, Mr Rogers, but Greg called me a Paki."

I was anticipating that Mr Rogers would react and discipline Greg for his racial insult. However, I was astonished to find I was met with silence.

Mr Rogers looked at me, turned right back around to the blackboard, and continued with the lesson as if nothing had happened. I was devastated and deeply disappointed with both of them. This double blow was twice as hard and twice as painful. Everyone is an influencer, and silence gives consent to undesirable behaviour. So there *was* a conspiracy—my parents were right. The "whites" were all in this together.

Indeed, the power of racial abuse over me was so imprinted in my mind that twenty years later, when I had just moved to Geneva in 1992, one of my husband's friends suggested we all go out for dinner and show me around the town. They discussed where they should take me.

"I know. Let's go to the Paki district!"

My heart sank. *Oh my God,* I thought to myself. *They have that word here too!* Little did I know that Pâquis[6] (pronounced "paki") is a cool eclectic area in Geneva with lots of cool restaurants and not at all a racial slur.

Home life was equally turbulent. I had gotten "accustomed to" intense levels of high anxiety and tension at a very young age. Anger, viciousness, fury, and rage were regular occurrences at home and a staple of my childhood. I had developed a thin skin, sensing everything more deeply than the others. The conflict in the family, the complications and the trauma, made it harder for me to feel relaxed

---

[6] The word *Pâquis* derives from the French word *pâturage*, meaning pasture, from a time when the area was just meadows located outside of Geneva. Today, the Pâquis district is lively hub for foreign cuisine and nightlife.

with relationships in groups and indeed with myself. My instinct, no matter how hard I tried to fight against it, was self-preservation. Looking back, I realize that I did not feel safe at home and did not feel safe outside.

I now know from my understanding of neuroscience that my brain was in overdrive, proficient from a very early age to be in survival mode and look out for danger, perceived or real. I remember feeling defenceless, voiceless, and vulnerable. Indeed, by the age of eleven, I was told by teachers at school and my father at home that I would never make it and that I would end up being a nobody, a nothing. And our child brains take in whatever is fed to them. On a regular basis, I would be given these negative messages which became part of the web established beliefs, the webs which trapped me:

> "You are stupid."
> "You are a problem child."
> "Why can't you be more like your siblings?"
> "You will never achieve anything."
> "One thing is for sure: you will fail in life. That I am certain of."
> "You? You could never do that. You're not clever enough."
> "You'll be a prostitute."
> "Write it down on a piece of paper that you will be a nothing, a nobody, a zero, and I will sign and date it."

These messages became a toxic mélange of judgements that darkened my dreams and hijacked my hopes. As a child, I found it difficult to push back and stand up for myself. No one at home knew that school was hell, as I was dyslexic, and no one at school was aware of how tremendously challenging my home life was. I remember to this day trying so hard at school to focus but with no luck. As a child, you just want to fit, and when you have a learning disability that no one is aware of, you stick out like a sore thumb. From my understanding as a former primary schoolteacher, I know that dyslexics experience unpredictable levels of emotional pain. This can manifest as low self-esteem and self-doubt.

Children are not able to disassociate themselves from events, as they feel have some responsibility. And as I have seen in my previous job as a teacher, children are also resilient. I certainly found ways to endure the drama. Nonetheless, it left a mark, and as a teenager, and consequently as an adult, I suffered from long stretches of angst, depression, and low self-esteem. My fear detector was always in high-warning mode, and I had to relearn the difference between real and perceived fear.

Fear and the anxiety that accompanies it are insidiously installed in our lives. For many years, my life, like the title of this chapter, was a forest fire—overwhelming, out of control, and damaged. As a consequence, I would do anything to be noticed—good, bad, and ugly. I recall during one of my escapades, my parents' close friends told my mother, "Aap ki larki apko tara dikahigee Rani." Translated, this means, "Your daughter will show you stars—not the good ones, but the kind that make you dizzy and out of control."

And I did. Rebelling was a symptom of not knowing myself. And this I know for sure: I was perceived within the family and in my community unit as a let-down, a disaster, a disappointment. I carried this guilt, shame, and anxiety into my adult life, which became a self-defeating and discouraging inheritance, until I got out of my own way.

By some wonder, I kept my faith by holding onto to any PPS (powerful positive statement) I heard. One such cherished PPS was from my favourite all-time film, based on the novel by L. Frank Baum, *The Wonderful Wizard of Oz*. This was one of the customary films shown every Christmas during the 1970s in the UK. The character I loved most was Glinda the Good Witch. I actually got to play her in our school production when I was ten and had the chance say those immortal words: "You've always had the power, my dear. You just had to learn it for yourself."

These words had such a pronounced influence on me. It was like a beacon of hope that things could and would be different for me. When I look back, I see that I scoured for mentors everywhere—in books, in teachers, in acquaintances, and in groups—and their words and models of behaviour gave me hope, which always left me with a feeling that things would get better. My life would be better. It was just a matter of time.

Full disclosure: I am only five feet two (155 cm for those who prefer metric), so you can imagine that I am tiny, yet I still got in my own way. The deep-rooted messages, the redundant voices, and the useless opinions all contributed to limiting myself as a person, as a mother, as a wife, and as a woman. My brain was addicted to drama, and I fed it diligently. I acted it out instead of working it out. The trauma of difficult past experiences shapes the brain and its reactions, yet trauma is not a prerequisite for feelings of low self-esteem. Once I got back in the driver's seat, I educated myself. I went back to school and attained a master's degree in HR and coaching to be better operationally and ready for the market. I was petrified and very worried about being inadequate amongst my peers, but I told myself, *No, don't stop yourself from doing something just because of the fear of failure.*

Consequently, I believed the fundamental message from my childhood that the *other* was more important. The *other* in my particular case were my parents, my siblings, my community, et al. Thus, my connection and the empathy I had for the other was very profound and far greater than the compassion and love I had for myself. By showing such empathy was the only way I could be *seen*.

Thus, I repeated this pattern unconsciously for many years before I made a conscious choice to untie each story that I had ever been told. Indeed, parents are the primary template as to how you relate to other human beings, and they are going to have an impact. However, once I became aware or conscious of how my parents influenced my decisions and relationships and of the things that held me back, I started on a path of reconciliation, creating new behaviours and new patterns.

These stories permeated my insides like a deadly cocktail made up of every painful event or message. Until I consciously countered them, they always came back to bite me, when I least expected it. And I noticed that whatever we fight gains might. Once I started to accept and become an observer of myself, I started to feel genuine appreciation for where I came from, what I had accomplished, what I had to overcome to be where I am now, and how I could help others. I quite simply got better at recognizing my emotions before they spiralled out of control and took control of me. As a result of this personal arising, my work flourished, my relationships transformed, and I discovered that, yes indeed, life was for living!

Fast-forward to the present day. I now run my own executive coaching consultancy, Walk the Talk. I coach, consult, and train all over with some of the most prestigious companies in the world. Moreover, I get to meet wonderful people and share something very deep with them.

> Think about it—even if you fail, you will learn from it. You will always get something out of it. And failure does not mean the end of the world. The new experiences and knowledge that you gain will lead you to something better, something that you're meant to be doing anyway. If something doesn't work out, there is a reason for it. Find the reason, and go with your intuition. Every time I have gone against my intuition, it has come to bite me on the bum (not a business term) when I least expected it!

But you know what the greatest part is? I get the unbelievable opportunity to support people in getting out of their own way. I get to witness people's transformation and be part of their path, and I feel so very privileged. I am very encouraged by the extraordinary people I meet.

I have learned so much from my work and from my clients, which is extremely rewarding.

Maybe my own story has shaped my career as a giver and as a supporter. Perhaps this is my meaning, what I was meant to do with my life. It certainly feels like my higher purpose and the reason why I am here on this earth. My trajectory of feeling, like that of an outsider, undoubtedly set me on a life purpose to bring all the outsiders into the in-group and give them a sense of belonging.

What I know is true is that we all experience this feeling. The feeling of not belonging, when we aren't good enough or we aren't truly accepted, is something we all feel at times to varying degrees, but it can also be something that we feel uneasy admitting to.

I can now see that this challenging period was indeed a gift, and please, let's be candid here: it has taken me a while to actually say that with genuine authenticity. The upside is that I now embrace my difference, and in turn I encourage others to be more compassionate about acknowledging others' differences. I can say that all these events have truly made me the person I am and have shaped how I relate to people. I believe that it has helped me profoundly to connect with my clients, to fully see them, to hear them, and to offer them true care and empathy. I realize that the adult people around me did the best they could with the resources they had. From a Hindu perspective, you are born with what you need to deal with, and if you just try to push it away, whatever it is, then it's got you! Hence, the practice of appreciation has become very significant in my life as I have witnessed first-hand that gratitude is a real motor in our well-being, both for those who cultivate it and for those who receive it. In my mind, forgiveness and gratitude go hand in hand. Forgiving is sometimes an arduous act, yet I have seen in my own life that it allows one to expand more.

The truth of the matter is this: whether you're a good person or a bad person is simply a story that you tell yourself. Now, cut yourself some slack while you're on a new learning curve. Recognize that we all make mistakes. When you forgive yourself and others, you are not pretending as though the transgression never happened. On the contrary, you are acknowledging that actions have consequences. When you do not forgive others, and especially when you don't forgive yourself, you remain in victim mode. But the consequences need not include self-inflicted negative feelings. Learn from the event. Finally, take the positive lessons from the experience and move on.

Once I had learned what my patterns were, what beliefs and which parts of myself I needed to work on, I was able to let go of the anger towards myself and know that the next relationship would be really different because I will have changed. I have often been asked this question in my own life: "Can we forgive the other, the one who wounded us?" I understand that to forgive is to release a gigantic mass of emotional baggage that we carry. To forgive is to liberate ourselves from that burden. What I recognize now is that we are all impacted by early subconscious messages that contribute to who we become and how we show up at work, at home, and in life.

When I felt wounded, I found it difficult to sustain the attachment, as the underlying fear of being let down, hurt, and scorned predominated my life. And we don't have to have major trauma in our lives. We all have internalized messages. It's part of the human condition. These voices come from teachers, siblings, and bosses. It is how you perceive the voices and how you adopt them that can influence how you behave. Did you work it out, or did you act it out? Are you still acting it out? The reality is that, for the most part, we are neither peaceful nor panicked. We are both at the same time. We all bear emotional injuries. They are as much a part of life as our physical ones, except we tend to take the latter more seriously.

The fear of disapproval can undoubtedly fill us with angst, but we know it's OK to make mistakes. It's all right for people not to approve of all our choices and for us to have feelings and struggles. But the truth of the matter is that we need to cut ourselves and others some slack.

When you truly forgive yourself, you are not pretending as though the past never happened. On the contrary, you are acknowledging that your actions have consequences. However, the consequences need not include self-inflicted negative feelings. You can learn from what happened. I still *like* approval. Who doesn't? But I don't *need* the endorsement of others, and once I understood that and learned how my webs kept me trapped, I was able to let go and be free.

Summary

- What are you still working out?
- What do you need to forgive yourself for?
- Hit the breather button daily.
- Remind yourself what you have to be grateful for.

Coaching Story: Donna

Donna had attended a leadership retreat, and the feedback from her peers and the facilitator was that she needed to work on executive presence. She felt the feedback was spot on as she was not being taken seriously at times in high-level meetings. I have noticed that in my work, women are often not shown how to develop executive presence before they start their careers. Typically, people who have executive presence exude self-assurance, composure, and influence. They intuitively know how to bond with others. What's more, they develop their individual strengths and are comfortable with their authentic self.

I noticed very early on that Donna gave very little eye contact, yet her voice was confident and unwavering. Her lack of eye contact in our first meeting left me wondering what impact this may have on others. We discussed what Donna's definition of executive presence was.

"I know my contribution to the organization is highly appreciated and valued. My boss advised me to develop my executive presence to further my career path in the company."

I asked Donna, "What would you like to get out of the coaching?"

I have found that focusing on the objectives is the best way to ask the client what would be most useful so as to look more deeply into what she wants and what she needs. The question leads to a comprehensive range of other questions and brings perspective and possibilities.

I sensed that Donna had self-confidence, and she transmitted this through a strong sense of authority, albeit without charisma. I shared a definition of executive presence from author and leadership expert Sylvia Ann Hewlett. "Executive presence is something what you signal to the world, you transmit to the world." According to Sylvia, developing this skill in leadership is not impossible, as much of it is very learnable.

"How are you signalling executive presence?"

"By being the best at what I do."

"What does that look like, being the best at what you do?"

"Always showing up, always being in control, not letting anyone too near me."

"What energy does that exude?"

Donna paused.

Being conscious of your energy and its impact and making sure you are aware of people and that people are aware of you are all aspects of executive presence. The hitch is that women seldom do something without feeling 100 per cent assured. So, I asked Donna, "Think about the leader you admire. What does he or she do to radiate executive presence?"

She paused again and reflected for a moment.

"Isabelle, my old boss, she was authentic. She always looked at me

when she shook my hand, and she put her other hand on my arm. I felt
the warmth and care from her." Donna was touched when recounting
her story. "But she also gave me authentic feedback. She did not try
to save me from the truth. Somehow, I did not mind. I trusted her
judgement. I felt safe."

"Is that what you would like to exhibit as a leader?" I asked.

"Yes. And I realize I am not doing enough of it. I recognize that
for my team to be bold, I need to let them know I am there. I need to
let them know that I have their backs, and I have to create the right
environment for that."

We looked at ways in which Donna could show more executive
presence: punctuated practice, regular reflective moments, journaling,
asking for feedback from trusted colleagues. And over time, the more
she practised, the more easily it became part of her. She had to do the
work to see the change.

My belief is that sharing intuition and insights is one of the
greatest gifts that coaches can give those their clients, provided they
have created safety. Sometimes I have been hesitant to share my gut
feeling, but every time I have, it has been a learning experience for my
client and for me.

**How to Get Out of Your Own Way: WEBs (Well-Established
Beliefs)**

Spiders don't get trapped in their webs as their victims do. Instead,
spiders move hurriedly and efficiently across their webs. Similar
to a spiderweb, well-established beliefs act as a method to catch
their victim, which in this case is us. These WEBs feel real even
though they may be dated. Furthermore, they command our
nervous system and thus authorize our feelings.

Which WEBs are you holding onto?
Which WEBs are useful?
Which WEBs are harmful?

Breaking the WEBs

Which WEBs are you prey to?

How are these WEBs getting in your way?
Journal your responses, and you will start to see a pattern, a repetition.
The next step is to examine your notes with a trusted friend, partner, advisor, or coach—anyone who will give you genuine, authentic, and productive feedback.
Develop and implement an action plan.
Be consistent and persistent. Then check in with somebody to keep you on track.
Which WEB still entraps you?

A web can be defined as "a complicated pattern of connections or relationships, sometimes considered as an obstacle or a danger".[7]

Go to the journaling section on page 130.

Note any thoughts and opinions.

In what manner are you getting in your own way?

---

[7] "Web", *Collins Dictionary,* https://www.collinsdictionary.com/us/dictionary/english/web, accessed 22 February 2019.

Chapter 2

What Have I Done to Deserve This?

> We realize the importance of our voices only when
> we are silenced.
>
> Malala Yousafzai

I don't know how to I got into university. I failed most of my exams at school. I even got a U (Unclassified) in English, the lowest of the low. Nevertheless, being dyslexic, I developed an unparalleled photographic memory to get through my exams. In addition to leading me to memorize pages of information, dyslexia forced me to develop my auditory skills, which became pretty damn good. Likewise, I worked incredibly hard, as I had a deep need to prove that I was not stupid and thick. Moreover, education amongst immigrant families was our insurance. There was always a sense that everything could all be gone in a flash, taken away without rhyme or reason. As a result, I developed a solid inner resolve, along with the deep fear that everything we had could be removed.

> Fear, I have seen, in my own life and in the lives of others, can be both positive and paralyzing. In extremes, these are equally dangerous.

My parents would often remind me when I was growing up that there are three things in life that are important: education, education, education. And nobody can take that away from you.

I was blessed to have studied psychology at university. I did not intentionally choose to study psychology. It was a very unusual choice for an Indian, as most of my peers at that time were fixed on the archetypal degrees—medicine, dentistry, law, and accountancy. My parents were so relieved that I had gotten into university. It meant that I would get a decent job, and of course education can never be stripped from you. Likewise, in the 1980s, the semi-arranged-marriage system still existed in the Indian community in the UK. Indeed, it was easier to get a "good matrimonial match" if you had a degree because university-educated women were definitely more marketable than non–degree holders. Once in a while, a match would come my way—an offer, an enquiry if I was available. It always surprised me the irony of how my *two* worlds operated in parallel and were so contrasting. One day I would be writing a psychological paper on women's changing role in society, and the next I would be dressed as an Indian bride in a glittering sari, being *exhibited* to a prospect. My mother was so concerned about my marital future that at any opportunity she had, at weddings or other social gatherings, she would stalk for an appointment with the official matrimonial matchmaker. FYI, the official matrimonial matchmaker was just a regular bloke with no magical matrimonial powers. Indeed, I saw many uncles and aunties (in Indian society, all elders are called "uncle" and "aunty") who had normal jobs during the week, working in the supermarket or in an office, and then miraculously turned into gurus, priests, matchmakers, healers, and astrologers in the evenings and at weekends. It was a mystical and miraculous form of moonlighting.

On one occasion, my mum ran into the most sought-after matchmaker in North London, to whom she pleaded, "What am I to do with an unmarried daughter? Please find her someone. Anyone."

"Raniji, she will have no problem finding someone. Don't fret."

"She won't, ji. She needs help! I know she is short, but she is so gori" (having fair skin; Indians are extremely colour-conscious, and being gori is huge plus for a girl in Indian society when looking for a suitable boy). This was all said in front of me, by the way. I wondered, was it her or indeed me who needed help?

While prowling around North London for a match, my parents would often remind me how liberal they were. "Vee are very liberal. You can marry anyone, but not black, white, or yellow—and no Muslims!"

"OK, so anyone from India then?" I answered sarcastically.

It was a running joke in our family that if I misbehaved, my marriage would be arranged to an African. Although seemingly senseless, this harmless banter and light repartee contained serious messages: stay inside your group and don't go outside of it, or else you will be barred from ours.

Inside, I told myself I was more than what people said I was and that I would find my own husband, not one who had to come to meet me with his parents' approval.

Indian weddings were always an enigma to me. Filled with colour and contradictions, pomp and show, they always attracted an audience who provided comedic moments. While watching the wedding ceremony performed on a stage, or mandap,[8] six hundred "close" friends and guests would sit sipping cold drinks and talking about the couple.

"She looks very Indian today, but I heard she was living with a white man."

"*Aacha?* Really?" said guest number two, throwing peanuts into her mouth as if they were going out of fashion. "And I heard the boy's parents are divorced."

This was completely customary—to judge, to disparage, all the while with the guests trying to make themselves bigger while making others small.

After I finished my degree, my mother eventually got her way and set me up on an introduction meeting with Vishnu. She had gotten

---

[8] A mandap is a structure temporarily erected for the purpose of a Hindu wedding. The main wedding ceremony takes place under the mandap.

the call from an "insider" (someone in the extended family, always a more popular option, as it was easier to check credentials and so forth). Vishnu was planning to come to see me with his father on a Saturday afternoon. My father reminded me before Vishnu's visit, "We are very liberal and very open when it comes to finding your life partner. Just no whites, no blacks, and no yellows—anyone from India is acceptable."

An hour earlier, I got ready upstairs, in a blue georgette sari, slightly hung over from the night before, having met friends in Reading. I had explained to them my predicament, and one of the guys there, Jasmeet Sehmi, jokingly said, "If it works out, please do invite me to your wedding."

I looked at myself in the mirror while getting ready. "What am I doing? Who the hell am I? Where is my voice? Why can't I say no?" The only power I had over the situation was that I negotiated with my mother that if I was interested in Vishnu, I would not eat a thing, and if I wasn't interested, I would attack the high tea she had so carefully arranged.

Vishnu arrived, escorted by his father. We all sat down, and Vishnu's father kindly invited Vishnu and me to get to know each other.

"*Chalo beta*, go and talk in the kitchen about your studies. Get to know each other." He chuckled like a proud father-in-law-to-be.

"You know, *Beti*" (Daughter) he turned to me—"I am very liberal."

Vishnu got up, but I did not budge, as I was too busy stuffing my face. At one stage, my mum stopped me in my tracks and beckoned me into the kitchen. I walked after her obediently with my mouth full of samosa, and my father followed suit.

"*Vah vah*, Rani! He's wonderful boy," my father announced proudly.

"Gulsuna." This was how my mother referred my dad, never by his name, as it was disrespectful for a wife to call her husband by his first name; ironically, calling him "oy" or "hey, listen" wasn't! "Sunita ko pasand nahee hai" (Sunita doesn't like him).

"Haiorraba! Kya? Kyoo? But I like him, Rano!"[9]

My father immediately turned to me and snapped, "Badtameez bevakoof Ki bacchii![10] What's wrong with you? He's such a good boy from a good family. You won't get anyone better than him. You can't afford to be choosy. Look at you and look at him. Who do you think you are? You are a nothing."

"Prove him wrong," I saw my mother mouth to me before my father stormed off. And I spent the next twenty years of my life trying to do just that, to prove myself. I was not alone. I have seen in this so many times in my life and in my work. When men in authority reject women, we interpret this as being "put in our place".

My saving grace was my degree. It was my safe place. The whole field of psychology was so much more than I had expected. It opened a new world for me, and I finally got some sense of why we human beings behave the way we do. My interest in and work on diversity (although, it was not called that then) began at university, and thus my thesis paper looked at the very problem of perception and stereotyping within minority groups in southeast England. My investigative attention was focused on the stereotyping of the minority group of themselves. The reality of stereotyping is that at times we can make devastating judgements based on only minimal information.

I understood that. Whoever we are and wherever we are from, we all have a predisposition to look outwards for our sense of well-being and affection, a need to be soothed, to be included, to be acknowledged. I wanted to do the opposite. I wanted us to look inward, to look at ourselves before we looked at others. Because the more we can locate well-being and affection inside us, the freer and more open we can be.

---

[9] *Hai rabba* means "Oh my God."

[10] *Badtameez bevakoof bacchi* means "shameless idiot".

One of the strongest PPSs (positive powerful statements) I received was from my psychology teacher Sarah Harrison when I was nineteen years old. As we all sat down ready and eager on our first day, she told us all in her opening/welcome speech, "You are in control. Nobody and nothing can control you unless you give them or it permission."

Most of us have pivotal moment in our lives. This was one of the first for me. I remember time stopping at that point and everything being incredibly still. That was a defining moment for me. Up until that point, I had not considered that I had any influence to control anything in my life, let alone myself. The inner voice, that voice in the back of my mind, was the material for all my conduct. All the WEBs had affected how I reacted to situations and how I behaved in the past and in the here and now. I had allowed people to control me and had allowed contexts to define me, and as a result I had been caught and trapped by my own well-established beliefs.

My takeaway was that it is not what happens to us in life that defines us; it is how we react to our life's events. I realized that when I placed my responsibility on other people, I gave away my power. I sanctioned them to disturb my joy, making myself helpless and powerless. I grew up in a home where there was a lot of confusion and chaos. I had parents who were individually deeply unhappy, preoccupied, and lost. They didn't know what they were doing or where they were going.

Summary

- Turn up.
- Turn on.
- Listen in.

Coaching Story: Jacinda

Jacinda was a successful life coach who came to me seeking support for how to brand or market herself effectively. She wanted to expand her clientele and services from individuals to groups.

As we began the coaching, I noticed that there was a discrepancy between where she was in her life and where she wanted to be. We both agreed to look at some of the limiting thoughts and limiting patterns to break through whatever barriers had prevented her from getting where she wanted to go. In my experience, you have to help yourself before you can help others. I always use the analogy of the flight attendants' safety message to the passengers when the aircraft is about to take off: "Put your oxygen mask on first before you help others."

Once we had established how we would like to work together and that this was her space to experiment, explore, and examine, we were ready to go.

"I'm in transition, and I don't know what that means for me to get back onto my path."

"So, what does that mean, 'get back onto my path'? And what would that look like?"

"For me, it is helping people to feel different, helping them make the shift. I want to help women and men on all levels. It's important for me, especially women."

"I see. So helping women and men on all levels is important for you. Is this what you are currently doing now?"

"No. I think I have the training, accreditations, and experience, but I'm uncertain how to go forward and transition into my new phase."

Interestingly, Jacinda required certainty in herself about what she wanted, and her doubt came out in her energy and created a reservation in prospective clients. We revisited her limiting thoughts and limiting patterns.

"I don't know. I can hear myself speaking, and I can feel that people listen, but they don't want to follow me because I am not certain of what I am saying. My core energy, my body language, my tone, everything, emphasizes my qualms."

"What happens to your energy?"

"I used to worry so much about how I was coming across. I feel like the spotlight is on me. When I work with clients, they say similar things, and I know exactly how they feel because I am in the same boat."

"Let's get back to you. Is that OK?"

Jacinda nodded.

"When you start promoting yourself, the spotlight is on you? Is this when you are one-to-one or in groups?"

"Most definitely in groups. This is where I feel the attention and the tension!"

When we are going through any personal or professional change, we are forced to see that what worked in the past may not work for the future. The assembly of people was a great contributing factor as to why Jacinda felt terrified. I suggested that Jacinda attend events, learn new skills, and keep abreast of what was new in her field to help her feel she was the real deal, because she was. I said that perhaps she should look for opportunities to speak publicly in a safe environment, low-risk to start with. I felt there was a strong link between her loss of dynamism in the presence of clients and her confidence.

Asking people to walk with you on their journey requires poise and presence. Jacinda really travelled from our first session until the end. Once her actions were clear and in place, her self-promotion and her wish to work in groups became smoother.

How to Get Out of Your Own Way: Emotional Audit

Observe frequently and write down how others influence your reality.

What are your triggers? What elicits anger, irritation, and anxiety?

I invite you to answer the following questions. It is what I like to call an emotional evaluation. I do it myself. It takes less than a minute. When I don't do this, I plummet right into a headless reaction.

1. What am I thinking?
2. What am I feeling?
3. What do I want now?
4. What do I need to do differently now?
5. How am I getting in my own way?
6. What PPS do I have to counter the jellyfish sting?

Drop your expectations. See people for who they are, accept where they are in their development, and focus on your own development. You are no longer inferior or superior. Just be.

Go to the journaling section on page 132.

Note any thoughts and opinions.

In what manner are you getting in your own way?

Chapter 3
Dancing in the Dark

Everyone shines, given the right lighting.

Susan Cain

There was a time when I took everything personally. I would hear, see, and feel things around me, pick them up, take them home, and make them my stuff. And, boy, it got heavy carrying all that stuff around. What goes in has to come out, and this heaviness manifested itself within me as anger or fear. It was my instinctive reaction to make everything about me. Both anger and fear, unlike joy and sadness, are emotions that create a divide. I crafted that divide by being distrustful and defensive, especially with the ones who loved me most. Most of us are skilled in conditional confidence. We can feel good and assured when things are going well, but we battle to stay inspired when things are difficult. I have seen in myself and in some of my clients that we are so very hard on ourselves when we make a mistake. We are more critical, more judgemental, and tougher on ourselves than we would be with anyone else.

What I have come to appreciate is that when others disapprove of us or criticize us, it frequently is not about us. However, if it is, we should take it as an opportunity to learn, to develop, to be luckier. I endeavour to be grateful that life presented this opportunity to me.

I appreciate it, perhaps not immediately, but I take the time to grasp the gift with both hands.

Once we assume and adopt other people's opinions that do not belong to us, a toxic resentment results, a deep frustration that we have created for ourselves. We internalize everything that is said as if it were *our* own thoughts. Slowly but surely, after I became weighty with the burden of all these superfluous statements, I got out of my own way by doing my own personal work. How? By recognizing that only I have the power to control what I feel, hear, and see—and nobody else!

In the very beginning of my career as an executive coach, I was invited by an archaic traditional Swiss bank to meet them, as they preferred a female coach. There had been a "beauty contest", as the bank called it, and I was one of the runners-up. The bank was a very old-fashioned, patriarchal, and conservative. One of the processes the company specified was that I was to go through the human resources team to check my credentials and experience. I went along one Tuesday morning, as requested, to meet human resources. When I entered the room, I saw that it was all white men on the one side of the desk and me on the other side. They were all millennials who clearly had no experience in coaching, and that was OK, but instead of owning it, they projected arrogance. Do you know how many times I have gone for a panel interview and been the only ethnic minority and the only woman? It has become the norm.

The conversation began badly. They were unprepared and had no idea who I was or why I was there. They openly admitted that they had not even looked at my CV, as they'd had more important things to do. They asked me how long I had been in Geneva and how I had gotten into the country. I was uneasy, and as a result, I stumbled when I replied in French. Eye rolls, sighs, and other disregarding micro-behaviours triggered my insecurities.

They were very disdainful with an attitude of superiority. I appreciate the idea of questioning a candidate to understand how much experience they have and what they can bring to the business, but to ridicule is amateurish, and incompetent interviewers reflect a miserable organization. The mood at the meeting was belligerent. The questions were ill-mannered, impolite, and coarse. I did try to empathize, and let me tell you—it is extremely difficult to empathize with someone who is being disrespectful and biased. Very soon, I realized that I wasn't getting anywhere as the conversation became more and more awkward. Consequently, I felt the old emotions rising inside me—I wanted to prove myself, yearned to show I knew my stuff. I had been shaken too many times, and I burst. Consequently, I went through all the customary amygdala hijack states: brain freeze, fight, and eventually flight.

When I left the room, I closed the door behind me. *What happened in there?* I thought. Was it because of me? Had I pressed their buttons somehow? What had upset them, and why? I was in victim mode, and try as I might, I could not get out of it.

I felt justified and looked for evidence to support my injury. When I got home that night, I wrote down how I was feeling. I asked myself the same questions I would ask a client:

What am I here for?

How can I rechannel the energy so that it will allow me to be free?

What and whom am I defending myself against?

I began to realize that when there was conflict, I would always take it personally. I was the target, and the other was the tyrant, thus making me emotional and unable to deal with the challenges at hand in a professional or productive way. I had difficulty distancing myself from the context, and my inability to perform effectively left me frozen. I took this interaction as a direct attack, which consequently impacted my behaviour adversely.

I lost the notion of being self-aware. I was asleep, and I lost myself. I realized that so many triggers had been activated—male authority, judgement, hostile behaviour, and exclusion. Unpacking my thoughts gave me a new kind of awareness. It was the uneasiness that was the hard spot, but it can be the most rewarding. I can't change people, but I can change my reaction. I saw that by becoming comfortable with anxiety, I could learn and do something different.

I wrote in my journal that day, "Lessons learned: I need to work on accepting that conflict is part of life and that I should not take it personally. Examine some deep-rooted beliefs about conflict. Build on my confidence, which is affected every time there is tension, stress, or conflict."

This experience made me realize my ego was in full combat mode. It was the singular driver of my behaviour. I saw that my ego was overwhelmingly powerful. It literally took over the real me, and my kindness and empathy got thrown to the wayside. This is all part of the human condition. We all have to adapt to situations; otherwise, we end up being resentful or frustrated. Watch your habits, observe your reactions, and by noticing, break the habits.

Ego is truly the absence of the knowledge of who we really are. This is especially true when we are in contexts we find challenging. I encourage my clients to notice what goes on for them emotionally, in their body and the thoughts they are experiencing in that moment. I came to this way of thinking, of consciously observing ourselves, through studying the work of the remarkable Eckhart Tolle. This was a great insight, one which allowed me to break harmful patterns. Tolle says when we connect with the deep "I", we are able to communicate without the need to prove ourselves, and we simultaneously strengthen our self-worth. Indeed, one of the most important lessons I have learned is that self-worth doesn't happen by osmosis.

Our challenge is to become more aligned internally with the existing moment, letting go of the need to triumph or the need to be accurate and instead focusing on the realities, the basics, the fundamentals. Every time we come back to the body, we come back to the present.

I noticed that that the ego at work and in other areas of life can become an enormous destructive driver in our behaviour. Besides this, the ego can be overwhelmingly powerful; it can literally take over the real you. This is something I have witnessed first-hand, as I am sure you have too.

When I coach groups of people, I encourage them to think of the bigger picture and not be self-centred. Play as one, not against each other. Building relationships is the key to success. However, relationships now go beyond the physical context as we live in an ever-changing world and are no longer defined by one set of rules. Our world is becoming increasingly relational and not transactional. We must also be aware that the most damaging relationships are the ones that go on for too long.

I see there is a difference between judgement and non-judgement. Judgemental statements are when you are evaluating someone or what they say without knowing all the truths. On the other hand, non-judgemental statements are when there is no approval or disapproval of the thoughts and feelings which were displayed by the people involved. They are normally supported with identifiable facts and measurable data. As you just read in the foregoing example, when my ego was not contained, it dissolved my authentic self in a split second, separated me from reality, and made me judgemental about others and myself. If you don't respect yourself, you invite disrespect.

I truly believe that this very awareness is an incredible source of wisdom that everyone can tap into. The true delight comes when we develop it and have faith in its direction. Nevertheless, too many of us fail to trust ourselves. Only when you sincerely heed to your understanding will you be able to gain a deeper comprehension of and compassion for others. You just need help in how to access it.

FYI, I was offered the job. The HR blokes checked my references with other, more senior men, and indeed they confirmed that I was a worthy coach. However, the unscrupulous interview made me think only once about taking the job. As I have seen in my life and in my work, an incompetent interviewer is a sign of an unprofessional organization. I had a choice and said, "Non, merci!" This was one of my milestone moments, knowing what was right for me.

Summary

- Break it down (thoughts).
- Break through (the old patterns).
- Break free (from old ways).

Coaching Story: Amy

Amy came to me through a referral. Her primary coaching need was to know more about her leadership and to develop her leadership style. She was a wonderful, wise woman with no end of experience.

I asked her who her leadership role models were. She spoke about her previous boss, who deeply cared about his people. He built trust with his team and his people from day one, and in particular he created trust and safety.

"How did he achieve this level of trust and safety?" I asked.

"He was an amazing leader, and I think he knew who he was and where he was going, so it was easy for him to lead."

During the sessions, Amy revealed she didn't know what to do and had somehow lost a sense of who she was as a person and as a leader. She felt that this affected many aspects of her life: her physical health, her career, and her relationships. She desired to explore what was getting in her way and to take purposeful action. I articulated to Amy that the motivation to change had to be greater than the motivation to remain in the same situation. I really wanted Amy to explore her personal passion and her true purpose, the one that energized her.

"Would you like to use this time to gain some perspective?" I asked.

"Yes. I need to take a step back from the day-to-day. I feel that everyone and everything is clouding my judgement. I want to reconnect with my purpose, reconnect in a meaningful way. I put so much pressure on myself. I have invested so much time at work, and my job is key to who I am. That doesn't feel right."

We worked together and reflected on what excited her, what made her connect with people, and where she wanted to go. After several sessions, Amy revealed, "Transformation is exhausting and a very intense experience! Before I ever started the work, I was so far from having a purpose. So much of our life is spent sleeping, and I was awake. I had felt a self-imposed pressure to succeed. I had just gone from one challenge to another. My energy has certainly changed. I was wiped out before, and I definitely feel now that I have a choice. I have the choice to respond differently to situations. My job is great, but it does not define who I am. It is part of me, not every part of me."

Subsequently, we worked together to truly identify what was critically important to Amy and then understand how she could apply her purpose to her workplace and her life.

Amy saw that to become an effective leader, one has to be aware of oneself and lead through example. In organizations, it is really important for leaders to connect with the people in their team to help them grow as humans, not just as employees. And if you are disconnected from yourself, it shows up in many different ways. Our coaching process allowed Amy to take a step back to indulge in some self-care. It was an oxymoron in that she felt self-centred for spending time on herself but also felt altruistic in that she was spending the time to be a better leader. The greatest gift for Amy was that she created the space to discuss confidential viewpoints in a safe and trusting environment. I always endeavour to walk the talk, and through compassion and kindness, I create trust and safety so my clients can talk about those hard topics and so that my challenging them does not feel menacing but rather seems like a realization or confirmation of their blind spots.

You see, we never know what is going on with people. We don't know what they are struggling with or what they are dealing with. Most people are not comfortable sharing real fears, especially at work, where they may feel judged and fear their image could be negatively affected. I hope that my coaching has a ripple effect and that once our coaching process comes to an end, it creates deep trust and safety for the people involved.

How to Get Out of Your Own Way: Ego—The Magic of Modelling NLP

When you intentionally study yourself and the people around you, you are showing a willingness to analyse and learn from your own experiences and also from the collective wisdom of those around you. If someone is producing good results around you, it should make you curious. Try to do what takes you closer to success, and enhance the behaviour that guarantees success.

People in this state are always asking a question of themselves—"What can I learn from people and situations around me?"

One process I use to invite my clients to achieve deep calm and silence is called **STILL:**

Still—Get yourself into a quiet and silent space internally, physically, and emotionally.

Timeout—Impose a timeout on yourself, a momentary interruption of your activity.

Impact—What power is this person or context having on you?

Let go—Break the thinking of what someone did, or didn't do, and release.

Listen—Listen to your body, your thoughts, your triggers, and your emotions.

When you're sensing a challenging reaction, the best thing to do is get still and stop.

What's one particular cue that comforts you, quieting your mind in stressful situations?

Go to the journaling section on page 127.

Note any thoughts and opinions.

In what manner are you getting in your own way?

Chapter 4
Freedom

Girls are taught to be perfect and boys to be brave.
Both are wrong.

Billie Jean King

Find a quiet place where you won't be disturbed and, just for a few minutes, think about how you would describe your leadership style. Dig deeper, and ask yourself: What type of person do I want to be? Where do I want to be? How am I going to get there? Am I really able to recognize my real strengths and weaknesses? Do I have a clear idea of who I want to be? What do I want to be known for? What legacy do I wish to leave? Can I identify the gaps? Do I really know myself as well as I thought?

When I work with my clients, what I really want to convey is that leadership is about being adaptable. At home, at work, and at school, leadership is about working with other people. It is about being able to deal with highs and the lows, and largely this has a great deal to do with understanding oneself. Working with my clients, I encourage them to become aware of their roles. Are they nurturing or directive? It may be a subconscious role, and by becoming more aware of it, they have the choice to decide if it will help them or hinder them.

Finding answered to these unanswered questions is where an executive coach can be incredibly valuable. Here is where an executive coach can boldly hold a mirror up to your face and help you truly confront and deal with those challenging issues.

An effective coach combines an enthusiastic intellect with a profound understanding of human nature. Therefore, coaching is an action-oriented process, focusing on the here and now, aimed at future impact.

The fundamental purpose of a coach is to commit to supporting her client and, through the coaching process, to enable the client to realize his or her own answers. It is the client who drives the process and who determines the goals. All the while, the coach will encourage the client to be responsible for her own development.

Change of any kind is stressful, and as a coach, one needs to be mindful of this. However, talking about your reactions can help you to deal with them more constructively. Indeed, I am attentive to how my clients feel, both consciously and unconsciously, and in turn how their feelings manifest in their fears and frustrations. And I like to remind the people I work with that when things aren't going well, they must give themselves permission to be human. When we acknowledge emotions, we are more likely to overcome them. Snubbing our feelings, positive or negative, leads to disturbance and sadness. The irony is that when we acknowledge our feelings, we give ourselves the go-ahead to be human and experience tender emotions, so we are more likely to open ourselves up to encouraging feelings.

There are numerous reasons for choosing coaching to work on difficulties, behaviours, or performance. Indeed, executive coaching can benefit those who want to develop their leadership and management skills and those who appreciate that their behaviour and their development impact the team and, in turn, the organization.

We all need help to put things into perspective, and it is not easy to self-evaluate. Therefore, having a coach brings an unbiased perspective to those internal conversations. A coach creates a safe space and can tell us certain things we don't necessarily want to hear. Although executive coaching has proven results and executive development is a critical aspect of all organizations, often it is only either called on in times of crisis or else neglected and seen as a nice to have rather than as a *must-have*.

Hiring a coach is the first step. The more you know about the coach, their process, and your goal, the clearer the decision will be. A skilled coach is both compassionate and competent, asking the right questions that trigger deeper reflection. They listen attentively without judgement. Everyone has different needs and their own personal goals, and thus coaches need to develop an individual approach towards each coaching assignment.

Before you meet your coach, reflect on the challenges you want help with, the outcomes you'd like to see. The sharper you are about your goals, the more you will progress in the coaching sessions and be clear about the motives for hiring an executive coach.

Each of the subsequent meetings should be focused on addressing your progress together with actionable feedback. Trust is an unconditional requirement between the coach and client; you must be able to feel you can voice any concern in the sessions. In my role as a coach, I help to identify, illuminate, and streamline which behaviours or patterns need to be developed to go to the next level. Besides this, I am always aware that trust and respect are very important to any relationship. Coaching is no different.

Coaching takes someone from point A to point B. Granted, the ride is not always smooth, but when you need direction, coaching is ideal, as it steers you back on track.

Coaching is an effective way to change something in someone's life that is not working. Indeed, coaching has a track record as a successful method to increase well-being, performance, and personal aptitude.

It has been shown to generate change, be it emotional, cognitive, or behavioural. Furthermore, research has shown that coaching can accelerate the attainment of specific goals by focusing on the competence of individuals in non-clinical circumstances.

Coaches are not hired to fix a situation. If a coach tells you that they can fix your situation, then don't hire them! This is a process that you have to work through, and it is hard work. However, if you do the work, it can be very empowering.

I believe this application is functional, as the coaching process offers guidance in a one-to-one relationship in which the coach supports the coached to identify, focus on, and achieve what is important to them. This is essential in this context because the client needs help to develop a career strategy and gain clarity. Coaches are there to develop a personalized approach towards your development. The executive coach emphasizes potentially hazardous topics that might impact interpersonal, strategic, and executive skills. Having clear outcomes is key to your results.

You determine what you *want* to attain by outlining clear outcomes. Then you begin to decide where you want to go and what you want to achieve. When you can act, you can begin to live your life with purpose and meaning. If you don't want to change, then don't waste your time or your money on coaching. Do it when you know you want to change. You are the driver, no one else, and it is you who will take personal accountability to authorize yourself.

When I work with my clients, I like to think of them as fellow explorers, highlighting that we are all in this together. I am not the expert. I am not fixed. I do not have all the answers. My approach is about creating a solid relationship with my client so we can investigate anything, securely and without judgement. Indeed, I truly struggled with putting up boundaries, especially because it was part of my script; to be seen and heard, I had to serve others. I often come across this question with my clients: "How can we responsibly uphold our boundaries?" It took me time to build boundaries for myself, and I now have seen that some of the kindest and most compassionate people have strong boundaries. Setting boundaries created a great learning opportunity and enabled me to gain insight and improve my daily mantra. It allowed me to reframe and tell myself a different story about the same events, leading me to accept that I am good enough.

Indeed, reframing is a central cognitive behavioural technique used to tell yourself a different story about the same events. I am very careful with the people whom I allow into my realm, and I have boundaries, which is strange because I could never manage to implement boundaries previously. Yet I now see that boundaries are vital not only for me but also for others.

Consequently, I started to notice the way people treated me and in turn the way I treated them. I started to observe that real affection is not controlling and not directive. It is accepting, supporting, and loving.

When I look back at my own career, I wish I had invested time in my own personal coaching. Sure, I have a close network of great friends and family, but an executive coach is impartial, experienced, and focused only on you. So, make sure you communicate with your coach about your objectives, and "interview" your chosen coach beforehand. There is a lot of work that goes into finding the right coach, but a good executive coach can make a huge difference to you, your team, and your organization. A good coach will be empathetic and tough at the same time by asking questions that trigger self-reflection.

Summary

Several questions to ask when you're in search of a coach:

- What type of coaching certification do they have?
- What type of coaching experience do they have?
- Do you they have any experience in psychology (which is suggested)?
- Have they worked with a professional in your industry before (that is, are they discreet)?

Coaching Story: Jane

Jane was the first female senior vice president with responsibility for a group of eight. The seven other members were all men, were from the same region, had similar university degrees, and knew each other well. She came from another domain, not having gone to the same university as the others and not having followed the traditional path to be a VP. When she came to our first coaching session, she was angry and emotional. She felt isolated and left out.

"I don't feel safe," said Jane. "It's horrible. I can't sleep Sunday nights because I worry about how the meeting will be. I practise what I will say and how I will say it …"

I played back the words and asked Jane what it was like to listen to what she had said. What was the impact of her state of mind on her work? I encouraged her to find here-and-now examples relevant to her interpersonal interactions. I know that being vulnerable can be scary.

"It sounds exhausting, Jane. Is that the case?" Jane nodded.

"Do you think the others are feeling similar feelings?" I enquired.

Jane reflected, and I gently encouraged her to be curious and let the matter rest, saying that we could rethink it later on.

"Can we dig a bit deeper into this word *safety*?" I enquired.
"Yes," Jane said.
"What's not safe? Give me some more colour to the context."

Indeed, challenging clients is essential in coaching. Otherwise, established patterns repeat themselves and never get resolved. I help my clients who are dealing difficult dilemmas to assume responsibility so as to shake them up into becoming aware of a certain behaviour pattern. But I give feedback gently with the positive intention that I wish for them to improve. I endeavour to be generous and positive, and I avoid empty compliments. In this case, it was my responsibility to encourage Jane to assume responsibility. Jane saw that the problems were outside herself. I encouraged her to describe a real-life situation at work and to look at her role.

"Every Monday we have the executive committee meeting with the CEO and the executive leadership team, but I cannot concentrate. I have my script ready in my head in case I get asked a question, but I feel judged. I'm not comfortable at all. I have a real fear that they are judging me."

"Is there trust among the team members?" I asked.
"I don't know. Maybe not, maybe so. I don't even think about it. I only worry about myself and how I come across."
"Do you feel part of the team?"
"Yes, I do, ironically. I know that I am in the right place, I have the right skills, and I don't feel like the poster girl or the token woman. It's more about safety."

We talked about the concept of psychological safety in teams. She had not heard this term before and was intrigued. So, I gave her an article to read for before our next session. The article, called "What Makes a Google Team Effective?", describes a series of interviews conducted with teams at Google. What they found was that there are five key dynamics that set successful teams apart. Number one is psychological safety. Fundamentally, this means that when a team has a high degree of psychological safety, they take risks without feeling insecure, embarrassed, or judged.

"I see that the processes and the content of our meetings could be so much riskier, more innovative, and definitely more creative if there were more safety. We are playing safe," Jane said boldly in our next session. "I sensed something but could not name it, and maybe I did not have the courage to call it out."

During the sessions that followed, Jane gradually came to an acceptance and understanding that the first changes she needed to make were within herself. She had thought about the concept of psychological safety and decided to take some responsibility and be accountable as the first step by talking about the concept with the group and outlining the benefits of psychological safety in teams.

"What I came to realise is that psychological safety is a shared belief. I can't do this alone. We all have to encourage each other to check in and challenge each other. What I was feeling was something everyone was feeling to some extent, but we all have different ways of managing and manifesting it. I noticed it and named it. This was the first step in helping to create more psychological safety."

Indeed, psychological safety means different things to different people. What is imperative is that its essence remain strong. That means that we all as team members create an atmosphere where people can show up and be themselves, and that is OK.

Once Jane had come to terms with what had to change, she dared herself, and in turn gave others in the team permission, to be different, act differently, and thus really get to the essence of what their purpose as a high-performing team was.

When our sessions were over, I shared the Glinda the Good Witch quote: "You've always had the power, my dear. You just had to learn it for yourself."

How to Get Out of Your Own Way: Reflection for Rewiring

Ask yourself the following questions, and answer them truthfully:

- What is it that makes it worth it for you even to consider changing?
- If things worked out exactly the way you wanted, what would be different?
- What are the pluses and minuses of changing and not changing?
- If this change were easy, would you want to make it?
- What makes it hard?

Part of the developmental process is reflective practice. This is a way of studying your own experiences to improve the way you act and react. The act of reflection is a great way to increase confidence and become a more proactive person. Engaging in reflective practice helps to improve the quality of people management.

It is a "sequence" because the action you take in the final stage will feed back into the first stage, beginning the process again. Following is the sequence:

1. Description—What happened?
2. Feelings—What did you think and feel about it?
3. Evaluation—What were the positives and negatives?
4. Analysis—What sense can you make of it?
5. Conclusion—What else could you have done?
6. Action plan—What will you do next time?

Go to the journaling section on page 136.

Note any thoughts and opinions.

In what manner are you getting in your own way?

Chapter 5
Here Comes the Rain Again

> I've talked to nearly 30,000 people on my show, and all 30,000 had one thing in common, they want to know; do you hear me? Do you see me? Does what I say mean anything to you?
>
> Oprah Winfrey

On Christmas Day 1991, my husband got a call from his cousin. His mother, while on holiday in Kenya, had been killed in a car accident. She was forty-seven years old. My father-in-law and my sister-in-law (only fourteen at the time) survived.

I had known my mother-in-law, Jiti, for exactly one year and one day. The last time I saw Jiti was at Geneva Airport in August 1991. She had come to send us off to London after we had celebrated our wedding reception in Geneva. She was crying when she hugged my husband. "Look after each other," she said amid the tears. From the few interactions I'd had with Jiti, I sensed she was reserved, restrained, and level-headed. Her strength was that she remained whole and true to herself despite what had transpired around her. Once we got the news, my husband frantically booked tickets, and then both of us flew to Kenya that same day. Christmas carols played at the airport, and turkey was being served on our flight as part of the festive season. I recall us arriving just in time for his mother's cremation as family members had held the body until he arrived for the son to perform the last rites. We were met by widespread sorrow, wails, heat, and the misery of it all, which consumed the family. It was a living nightmare, a family holiday that turned into a family heartbreak.

We had been living in London, but because of the family tragedy, my husband pushed our move to Geneva soon after. I had no idea how the family "should" grieve her death. I just knew that for my husband and his family, life had changed because Jiti was no longer there. I sensed that the family needed support. They needed a space where they would be able to share their grief. Undeniably, when it comes to dealing with grief, people behave in all kinds of startling and erratic ways, and that surely was true for all of us.

Most of their family friends would come to pay their condolences once and then not follow up or check in to see if the family needed anything. When it comes to grief, the grieving need people around them to enquire after them, to care, to be there, and to not be there. My in-laws felt both the loss and the loneliness. I think trauma is really tricky. All these emotions that one is supposed to feel do not necessarily flow in a straight line. Every emotion believed to be normal may come or may not, but in any event, there is nothing about grief that is easy.

My father-in-law said that when he was a child, death was handled with dignity. He told us that in Indian villages, the whole neighbourhood would come and visit the grieving family to let them know how much they felt the loss, and both the relatives and neighbours would make the bereaved family weep and would not leave the family's side. He said it was a form of psychotherapy and very healing for the heartbroken. This type of attention and deep connection requires people to have a deep sense of empathy, to fill the void and create an inclusive atmosphere of belongingness. Death and the whole subject of mortality fascinates me, as I see how they are so closely linked to living a fulfilled life.

In 1992, two months after my mother-in-law's death, I moved to

Switzerland from London. I found it difficult to settle into the Swiss way of life.

I attempted to join a women's network group and volunteer in the community to get my foot in the door, but it was all in vain. Moving abroad was challenging, and moving to another country because of a partner was a lonely experience. I felt like it was the first day of school and I had to start all over again.

I was having real difficulty in adapting to change, moving to a new place, and trying to develop new professional skills that aligned with the host country's market needs. I was left with a feeling of low self-worth and a longing to go back home. Looking back, I see now that I was dealing with loss and longing for my old, familiar life. Having no friends, no support circle, I felt childish and pathetic.

Finding the right job in a new context requires time, perseverance, self-esteem, and patience. It is very difficult to remain resilient and to remember that trailing spouses have acquired real valuable skills that can be transferred to many markets.

I knew that to regain my self-esteem, I had to develop skills that were in line with the market needs in Geneva while working on my own personal cultural adaptation to life in this new city. Moving abroad can be thrilling but at the same time a lonely experience for many trailing spouses who feel they have to start all over again by making new friends and finding a job. My move to Switzerland made me think about my parents' assimilation. I did not feel connected to my host country. I did not speak French, and I had lost my identity, constantly looking back to my old life and the country in which I had grown up. When I mentioned to anyone in London that I lived in Switzerland, I was always met with gasps of amazement and wonder. But the reality was that everyone and everything I knew was not in Geneva. Life was easy in London. I knew the place. I spoke the language. Here I had become dependent on my husband and his family for everything. I had no idea about life in Switzerland, and I was very lost. Every day felt like the first day of school. I could not speak a word of French, and the only phrase I could remember was "traverse la rue and devoir!" My experience helped me to help others and thus led me to write a very successful article in *InterNations Magazine* called "Following Your Spouse Abroad: How to Reinvent Yourself".

When I recognized that I was repeating the same behaviour pattern as my parents had, I decided not to go down that path. I really wanted to make Switzerland my home, and I wanted to feel part of the local society. Furthermore, I learned that expectations don't always match reality and that patience is indeed a virtue, one that I had to develop! Like before, when I was a young teenager, I started to search for mentors everywhere. I figured out that not only could I live the life that I wanted to live but also, I could also help others live up to their own aspirations. I understood that bringing the best out of people and helping them reach their potential was something I was born to do. I began to look forward to the fact that I could reinvent myself, starting a new life with new dreams and a new purpose! I had to create and build a new purpose despite all the sorrow around me. I guess it was a rebranding exercise, although I didn't know that at the time. So, I embraced the culture and did my best to integrate fast. I learned French, and with time, I figured out my own way in life. We really only get one chance, so I live life to its fullest.

As a consequence of my own life experiences, I have a deep sense that people, including myself, feel unsafe when they don't belong. Belonging helps us survive and thrive, and this has never been truer than in today's society and organizations.

> No matter what background, ethnicity, or gender, all employees want to belong. The need for belonging is a shared experience like the need for food and shelter.

My background has left me with a strong sense of being a connector, a bridge. In my work and in my life, I encourage people to acknowledge that we all have very similar needs, concerns, and hopes. How we connect on these likenesses is central to all human relationships. I have let this be my passion, my charioteer, and my purpose both personally and professionally. I like to think of myself as a guide on this journey of examination because I have visited this sphere many times before.

Getting out of your own way means different things to different people, but it is about all of us, wherever or whoever we are in the world. It begins with us. It's about knowing yourself and having a deep understanding of the other. It's a skill that we desperately need not only for home and work but also for humanity worldwide.

Have you ever put yourself in someone else's shoes and had the experience of seeing the world or situation through their eyes? Have you ever tried to be an observer, detached and balanced, looking at a situation as if you were not a part of it? Simply put, identification is the ability to recognize, understand, and share the feelings of another person, seeing the situation or world from their point of view. It is looking at a situation as an external impartial observer, dissociated and emotionally detached from the situation.

This perceptual position will enable you to have a balanced approach, especially in emotionally charged situations. You may step back and watch yourself. It is like seeing the situation on a movie screen. There are unconscious forces in us all that we should endeavour to understand. Once you know yourself, you can communicate effectively and consciously. This is a vital part of self-awareness. None of us are not stand-alone beings. We are part of a community, and when you recognize this, you become more in tune with your communication. Indeed, how you communicate with others is the single most effective tool you will need in your life.

Empathy is the capacity to understand the feelings and thoughts of another. It is not compassion or sympathy. Empathy is simply an essential element for living better with others. When you can put yourself in the other person's place to understand how they work, their thoughts and their emotions, then you can demonstrate true empathy. The supremacy of empathy is that allows us to understand each other, accept each other, encourage mutual understanding, and encourage mutual benefit without rescuing.

Let's be clear: empathy does not mean saving someone or being soft and fluffy. It is possible to deliver tough messages directly, respectfully, and empathetically as long as you are conscious and authentic. With empathy we can apply soft influence to bring about firm results. Thus, empathy is about being sensitive, caring, compassionate, and deeply concerned with the personal growth of yourself and others. That requires a deep dive to discover how your own conditioned beliefs and values that affect your behaviour. Thus, the essential universal skill is empathy, the capacity to truly understand what another person is experiencing from within. And indeed, to truly understand another person, we need to stand in their shoes. Through empathy, we discover how other people would like to be treated by us. We hear them, we see them, and our connection with them is deeper, richer, and fruitful. If most of our behaviour is unconscious, it creates blind spots and biases that constrict our vision. Without our conscious consent, these blind spots exude into our daily lives and shape our judgements and decisions when we least expect them. The biggest challenge, I believe, is how to create a strategy within the corporate culture that can truly change mindsets and challenge our deep-rooted beliefs. The real journey begins with you and me.

When Lady Diana died, the national grid recorded a power surge as millions of Britons switched on their TVs and kettles as the news of her tragic death spread across the nation. Hospitals throughout the country experienced an increased number of consultations for psychological problems as well as a larger number of admissions for trauma. What was it about Diana that made people feel so connected to her? I believe she had the gift of making other people feel seen and heard. What was it about Mother Teresa that touched us with her compassion and kindness? Legendary for her work, she devoted her life to caring for the hungry, the unprotected, the homeless, the crippled, all those people who feel discarded and loathed throughout society. What was it about Gandhi's deep empathetic instinct that made him look beyond religious boundaries? A devout Hindu, he openly announced, "I am a Muslim, and a Hindu, and a Christian, and a Jew—and so are all of you." These words, which still resonate with me today, are amongst the most ultimate empathetic declarations of all time, because kindness is the highest virtue.

I like to think of our global community as a kaleidoscope tube with plain mirrors and coloured-glass pieces at one end forming different patterns of different colours. When you look through one end and turn the tube, you see different patterns of all kinds of brilliant colour combinations. Kaleidoscopes make it possible to view everyday things in surprising ways. You are in control of what you see because you decide where to point the scope, but you are also unable to predict exactly what you will see—and you are often astonished by the boundless possibilities created by such a humble device. Psychologists have used kaleidoscopes as healing tools to revitalize patients' sense of purpose as well as to analyse the connection between human perception of symmetry and colour. I like to use the kaleidoscope symbol when I meet new people and new clients. It reminds me to see them as a kaleidoscope moment, a blend, a mixture, a medley, and thus accept the whole person for who they are.

Summary

- Take a mental or physical pause from any challenging context.
- Make a regular assessment of your state.
- Make sure that what you say is constructive.
- Let those involved know you care.

Coaching Story: Helene

Helene had been with her company for sixteen years. She was advised to receive coaching by her boss because he had observed (and learned through feedback) that Helene, a valued member of his team, found it hard to give actionable feedback. He believed that being a top talent meant that sometimes you have to give tough feedback that might not be deemed welcome or desirable.

Helene told me firmly in our first session that she did not believe she could change. Nevertheless, she was open and curious to know more.

Helene needed facts to be convinced, so we talked about capability versus congeniality and the body of work proving that the more successful a man is, the more he is adored. However, the more successful a woman is, the more she is loathed. Research findings have confirmed that while men are expected to be influential, self-assured, and accomplished, women are expected to be kind, understanding, helpful, and heartfelt.

One of the questions I asked Helene was "What's the difficulty for you here?"

Helene explained that within her team, there were a number of different personalities. Her role was to assist in their development. She felt focusing on their positive aspects created an atmosphere of harmony and congruence.

I asked her again, "What's the difficulty for you here?"

"Giving negative feedback. I just hate upsetting people, especially since we are all friends."

We looked at the word *negative*. How could we reframe it? How could we view this as an opportunity for her team member and for her? Helene agreed that providing feedback is one of the most important things you can do for your team, and her boss's feedback to her had been very helpful and constructive. We looked at how she could create a team culture where giving and receiving feedback became the standard and not something awkward.

Together we created a plan where she would seek opportunities to give recommendations and in turn ask her team for feedback, consistently and frequently, until it became the norm. Giving feedback is a skill and is learnable. When you give it with the purpose of helping the person to grow and flourish, it has a long-lasting promising effect on the individual. Giving feedback should always be with the intent of helping, and indeed helping is an essential human pursuit. We do it at home with our partners, our children, and our loved ones. We do it every day. We seek out help too, although all too often it's a practice that can be difficult to perform and accept. And at times, our earnest offers to help are resented and rebuffed. So why is it so difficult to provide or accept help, and in what way can we make the whole process easier?

Corporate culture and organizational development guru Ed Schein analyses the collective and psychological subtleties common to all types of helping relationships. In his book *Helping*, he explains why help is often not helpful and shows why any would-be helpers must guarantee that their assistance is both received and valuable. He suggests the following stages of enquiring to enable genuine support:

Always begin with humble enquiry.

Effective helping begins with readiness. By simply listening to the client's story, using "humble enquiry", as Schein calls the process strategy at this stage, the client begins to feel like there is a better balance in the relationship just by being heard. That begins the development of trust. "Be cautious not to fall into the diagnostic trap too early," he advises.

Experts are more comfortable with the kinds of questions that lead to solutions. "Who was at the meeting? When did you meet? What did the other party say? How did the language in that meeting compare to prior email communications?" Using those kinds of diagnostic questions too early may impede the development of the relationship. The quality of informed questions is an important factor in a client's decision, and informed questions tend to be diagnostic. Indeed, when I work with organisations, I always remind them that the three most important words in business are "Tell me more."

"Why did you choose this way?"

"Have you thought of some other alternatives?"

Start with process enquiry, and return to it often.

Schein uses process enquiry to describe the underlying process of relationship-building and problem-solving, not to focus on the substance of the problem. For example, the question "How would you see a successful outcome?" at the conclusion of an initial consultation turns the focus to the client's expectation of the process outcome. That question might uncover a discomfort with the unintended consequences. Occasional questions during meetings, for example "How can we better communicate about this topic?" and "How am I doing in keeping you informed?", turn the focus to the relationship, keeping it dignified between you and the other as input is sought, which in turn continues to build trust.

"Bad help means asking the wrong kind of questions," says Edgar Schein in his book *Helping*. However, by using the foregoing strategies, you can avoid giving the wrong type of help, whether at work, with your children, or with your spouse. I have found this book to be fundamental not only on a professional level but also on a personal one. I was very lucky, as I fell upon this book when my mother was diagnosed with cancer. The book helped me ask the right questions so that I could assist, care, and be present until the end.

How to Get Out of Your Own Way

Tips to Increase Your Empathy

It is possible to develop empathy towards others by using these three tips:

1. *Do not take account of yourself.* It is important to forget about your own principles, judgements, values, and beliefs, and all that can limit the understanding of the other, to really have empathy.
2. *Know how to listen.* Listening without interrupting the other person and asking questions about his or her perception of the world or the situation helps you to get to know him or her better. Remember that *silent* and *listen* have the same letters.
3. *Increase emotional understanding.* Each emotion can cause a lack and a different reaction from one individual to another.

Go to the journaling section on page 139.

Note any thoughts and opinions.

In what manner are you getting in your own way?

Chapter 6
Into the Groove

> It is said that girls with dreams become women
> with vision. One must work at it. Let us work at it.
> Together. Starting now.
>
> Meghan Markle

When was the last time you were in a conversation and you felt you were getting nowhere? We often find ourselves blaming the other person, or the context, for the absence of the desired result. Rather than looking at the outside, I have found it is more successful to go within. Literally observe yourself. Use the following IRIS model to guide you.

In Greek mythology, Iris was the goddess of the rainbow. She rode the rainbow as a multicoloured bridge from heaven to earth, the three petal segments of the iris flower representing faith, wisdom, and valour. IRIS stands for intention, respect, I-statement, and self-awareness.

Intention

Basically, this is your objective, your purpose, your goal. Most transactions break down when our intentions are not clear to the other party or indeed to ourselves. According to Gary Zukav, intention is at the heart of creating authentic power. Intention is something with a cause and an effect. You must be sure of your intent when you are communicating as this has a direct impact on the result. Once we are clear about our intent, we are clear about our message, our resolve, and our objective.

Furthermore, every choice we make, each deed we take, is intuitively born out of an intention. That is how powerful intention is.

> When our intention is not aligned with our genuine goals, then confusion, misunderstandings, and a breakdown in communication result.

Respect

Respect is unquestionable and is what most people crave from their managers and colleagues. People learn by example, so exhibit self-respect and respect for others. These two things are not mutually exclusive. This means being professional and direct but nevertheless respectful. Our world is becoming increasingly relational and less transactional, so to have real connection globally means we have to focus on the whole person, the entire person, the person who shows up, and not who we believe they are.

I-Statements

Thomas Gordon developed the concept of an I-statement in the 1960s. The intention of the I-statement is to create a protected space for clients to express themselves. Carl Rogers accomplished this by using reflective listening and self-disclosure and by demonstrating empathy and unconditional positive regard for the client. We now know that these methods can be used together in personal and professional fields. Furthermore, when we use I-statements, we are able to invoke the same emotive resonance in our professional relationships, leading to a richer connection and bond. Good communication is essential for building strong relationships, and without real communication, relationships can turn bitter and lead to scepticism and errors. The I-statements are an operational means of communicating since they conserve a humble attitude towards the receiver while enabling the speaker to say how he or she feels. When used correctly, I-statements can help foster positive communication in relationships and may help them become stronger, as sharing feelings and thoughts honestly and openly can help both parties grow closer on an emotional level.

Self-Awareness

Self-awareness is the institution of personal growth and success. Daniel Goleman calls it the "keystone" of emotional intelligence; indeed, building self-awareness is a lifelong effort. Interestingly when I talk about self-awareness in my training with clients, I see eyes roll, and I remind the cynics that if they are not aware as the leader of an organization, they should know that self-awareness is a soft skill that translates into hard results. Daniel Goleman reminds us that "self-awareness isn't just navel-gazing. It's the presence of mind to actually be flexible in how you respond. Also, it allows you to be centred, and know what your body is telling you." Self-awareness, he adds, is the ability to monitor our inner world—our thoughts and feelings.

Self-awareness is central because when we have a greater understanding of ourselves, we can experience ourselves as separate individuals. This then enables us to build on our areas of strength as well as detect areas where we would like to make developments.

Summary

- We are neither inferior nor superior.
- Do not see the other as the wounded or the oppressor.
- Our desire to help is directed by the other.

Coaching Story: Sangeeta

Sangeeta had been working part time since her children were born and felt stuck in her role at work and wanted more. However, Sangeeta, through her own admission, was not clear as to what that looked like. She spoke at length about her frustration with her current position, and simultaneously she spoke about the fact she had freedom and time with her two children. I noticed an incoherence and shared my observation with Sangeeta. Indeed, she proceeded to tell me that she had spoken to her line manager the previous week to negotiate a pay rise.

"It went terribly wrong. I wanted a salary increase and walked out with another project and less pay. I was so set on asking for what I needed and walked in with the aim to resolve the salary issue, and I walked out with two problems. More work, same pay!"

We looked at this situation together, and I asked her, "What happens when you ask for something for yourself?"

"I tend to speak long sentences that are disconnected. I feel that my peers have covered what to say and how to say it really well. I am not precise or clear. I just ramble on and on. I can actually see myself doing it and can hear myself, but I can't stop myself. When my boss asks me what's going on with an issue, I can't seem to get right to the core of the issue. So, he avoids me, or he asks me by email because it's quicker. I am doing it now."

Sangeeta had many anxieties about the impact of her communication and how it was affecting her image and influence at work. She often used minimizing phrases like "I am just a manager." She apologized a lot and often marked herself down. I emphasized the impact of her self-discounting, and I assured her that even the most successful people have fears, but they use strategies to deal with them. Some of the most successful people I have encountered know when they are wrong. That is a genuine asset.

I sensed that a great deal was happening for Sangeeta even before she even spoke. The inner noise was impacting her daily work and life. Consequently, we acted out various candid scenarios together through the power of role play. In my opinion, life is one big role play as we are constantly playing one or many roles.

Accordingly, sometimes she was in the hot seat, as I sometimes was. I tried to give her alternative approaches to dealing with situations, not providing recommendations.

This was a very powerful exercise for Sangeeta as she saw that her micro-behaviours had a big impact on others. And she could now see why. Her biggest takeaway was to be prepared before any major exchange and to say what she needed to say. She realized that if this was not possible, she should remind herself she did not have to say what she thought but rather empathize with what the other person might be thinking or feeling. That gave her the confidence and control that she needed to go forward.

How to Get Out of Your Own Way

Here are my guidelines which I have found useful for connecting with people:

1. *Care.* To care means to feel genuine concern and interest in the other while ensuring you look after them and provide for their needs.
2. *Compassion.* We all need to care about people, and we need to start with ourselves—that is we have to be compassionate towards ourselves and mindful of our needs and of the sorrow of saying goodbye to our old lives.

How and where can you use IRIS?

Go to the journaling section on page 141.

Note any thoughts and opinions.

In what manner are you getting in own way?

CHAPTER 7
What Difference Does It Make?

Power's not given to you. You have to take it.

Beyoncé

One of my dearest and closest childhood friends and I have had an annual minibreak since 1995, just the two of us together. Our bond is precious and very deep. We use this opportunity to support each other, discuss, divulge, and debate. This time for me is magical. She holds the mirror right up to me, as I do for her, and it is always with love and care. One time, our annual minibreak was planned in Paris. We sat down for dinner, and I suggested we do an exercise—to give each other feedback, real, authentic feedback, the good, the bad, and the ugly! I always recommend practising giving feedback in the language that is familiar to whomever one is giving feedback.

We asked the following questions: How did we experience each other on a one-to-one basis? How did we experience each other in a group? The deep trust we have in each other allowed us to take a chance and give authentic feedback to each other. In reality, this sort of thing shouldn't be hard to hear if you know yourself; however, how it is said is a different matter, and that is where positive intent is paramount. As both of us are freelance workers, we find it hard to get fully candid advice.

So, we established some ground rules: firstly, we were not

allowed to justify the feedback while the other was talking; secondly, we were not allowed to defend the feedback while the other was talking; thirdly, we could write down how we felt when we heard the feedback; fourthly, we would acknowledge the feedback. Layers serve a purpose. They protect us so we do not get hurt, and yet when we ask a trusted advisor for their honest opinion, unpeeling those layers, the result can be golden. The exercise was very meaningful for me, and although it was not always easy to hear the answers, I valued this precious gift. In fact, this listen-and-learn exercise is something my friend and I still do to this very day, and not only in Paris. Sometimes, like medicine; the feedback is hard to swallow, but we know we are going to feel better sooner or later. I encourage you to do the same with someone to whom you feel connected. Simply follow the rules and listen and learn.

In real life, it is not easy to be so candid, especially when the risks are high (e.g. in a professional context). We fear how the other person will receive the feedback. Therefore, feedback is a process that requires constant attention. When something needs to be said, say it. People then know where they stand all the time, and there are few surprises. Also, problems don't get out of hand. While formal feedback may be given infrequently, simple informal feedback should be given much more often—perhaps every week or even every day, depending on the situation.

You need to understand how to offer feedback effectively and model how to receive it productively. When you make a conscious choice to give and receive feedback on a regular basis, you demonstrate that feedback is a powerful means of personal development. Done properly, feedback need not be agonizing, demoralizing, or daunting—and the more practice you get, the better you will become at it. Indeed, the ability to receive feedback isn't something we are skilled at, nor do we truly appreciate the power of it. It is a key practice and a formidable device for contemplation, change, and enhancement.

Some reflective questions include the following:

- What are the possibilities?
- What might be the implications?
- How is the other person likely to react?

While working with a team of coaches, I once asked a colleague at the start of our coaching week together to give me feedback on how he experienced me as a coach. I did not know him very well, and I could tell from his initial question ("Why? You seem to be fine") that this was not an easy process for either party. I encouraged him to fulfil my request and asked if we could check in at the end of the week. He kindly agreed. The day came, and I asked him, "So, how did I do? What do I need to change?" He was very generous with his feedback and his time. It really helped me a lot. It got me thinking, *How could I use this for my clients?* I had found the exercise very powerful. Plus, I noticed in my own coaching work that people are either too hard-hitting in giving feedback or too distrustful in receiving it. I see more and more that giving and receiving feedback is a fundamental skill that we all need to develop.

Then, in 2016, I was traveling from Geneva to London for work. I stopped at London's Waterloo station to take an intercity train. While I was desperately trying to figure out my next departure time, I heard an announcement by one of the staff: "See it. Say it. Sorted."

It was a new nationwide campaign to encourage train passengers and station visitors to report any unusual items or activity. Designed by government, the police, and the rail industry, the campaign aims to raise awareness of the vital role the public can play in keeping themselves and others safe. This left me thinking, *What if we did more of "See it. Say it. Sort it" [my tweak]? What if we were not afraid to point out anything that felt out of place?*

If you, as a member of any organization, family, or institution, decide to give honest feedback and make sure the feedback is conveyed in such a way that others can acknowledge and assimilate the information, then you will have a group that keeps communicating with respect.

So then, what if we used "See it. Say it. Sort it" with each other with respect and care to help us keep all parties safe? When it comes to our blind spots, in other words, not noticing or accepting our behaviour, self-awareness is treasured currency, as is being open to feedback. This is true of all interactions, personal and professional. The more people I work with and meet with, the more I recognize how many experiences and emotions we share. Despite our cultural and geographical differences, we all embrace many commonalities. Yet life is so demanding that we often don't have time to be thoughtful as to how our behaviour touches others around us. What makes us forget these common denominators is often a feeling that we are the only ones going through tough times. That's the story we tell ourselves, and then others do the same, all of us creating a collection of stories. This rationale can become fixed in our thinking and in our behaviour, and this influences the way we interact with one another.

We are social animals. We learn from others by watching them, observing them, and learning from them. So, it takes one person who dares to speak up and break the pattern. Feedback is a real gift. Make sure to ask for it regularly and truly. If you are conscious of who you are, then feedback should not come as a surprise.

> One piece of advice: Don't give feedback when you are feeling irritated or heated. Trust me, it doesn't look pretty.

Coaching Story: Katina

Katina was promoted to executive director of a private bank after the previous advisor was asked to leave. Her role was to develop key relationships with "difficult" clients whom she had inherited from her previous colleague. Katina found that her interactions with these difficult clients were tiring and heavy, and she could not deal with situations of conflict. Katina worked in a very male-orientated profession. Many of the women around her were either assistants or receptionists. She was the only woman at the bank's executive level. Part of work life is managing not only one's own emotions but also the emotions of others.

The stakes were high, literally and metaphorically, and Katina often had to compete for her patch, either with clients, peers, or superiors. Managing emotions at work is about not only our emotional state but also that of others, and this was a challenge for Katina.

However, although Katina was tough (her own words) when there was conflict at work or at home, she would take these incidents as personal affronts, becoming emotional and unable to deal with the challenges in a professional or productive way. Katina was having difficulty distancing herself from the context. She could not perform effectively, as she would freeze in some interactions, as by her own admission she took the feedback as criticism or a direct attack. This negatively affected her behaviour.

Katina was very open, and she immediately told me that we needed to work on accepting that conflict is part of life and not taking it personally. It was a bad practice she wanted to get rid of. I agreed that Katina would benefit from getting help through coaching for how to manage conflict successfully. We looked at how people around her reacted to conflict. What made sense for them, especially at times of high stress? Did they even think about the impact? Did she care about her relationships at work?

I sensed that Katina suffered for being sensitive and perceptive, which manifested as being hypersensitive to "conflict" at work. She was often interrupted in meetings and held back ideas or suggestions, only to hear her male counterparts share the same ideas a few minutes later. Part of the conflict she felt was the anger she experienced by being the only female in a top position and having to prove herself.

"I feel so out of control at times. It's an old and bad habit," she admitted.

Through the sessions, we studied many ideas and explored what was going on for Katina when there was disrespect at work. She found that some peers' behaviour was disrespectful. It is important in coaching to really hear the client and respect their truth. I had not met her peers—I only knew them through the eyes of Katina—and thus my role was to hear her truth and the impact their actions and attitudes had on her. I asked her a question and recommended that she think about it. There was no rush, I said; I wasn't going anywhere.

"What habits do you need to break?" I enquired.

I encouraged her to note her reactions when she perceived there was disrespect at work. I recommended a type of self-audit. I suggested that she carry a small journal and write down what she was feeling. The overall message was to make herself a priority, to look, listen, and learn, and be cognizant of what was going on inside as well as outside.

A few weeks later, Katina came into the session with an idea. She had put a lot of pressure on herself, especially because she was operating in a male-dominated environment. I encouraged her to explore why she had put so much pressure on herself and where this originated from.

Katina did the work. She mentioned that she was very doubtful, but she took it as an opportunity.

"It's not about me, and I have made it about me. I noticed there are things I can control, my reactions, and things I cannot, like other people's behaviour. I don't agree with the way some people behave, and I get angry that they are allowed to be disrespectful. This is what pushes my buttons. Only I can break this vicious cycle and be free."

That was an aha moment for Katina. Full accountability and full responsibility mean liberty, and Katina realized that she needed to be fully accountable and take full responsibility in order to be free.

Summary

- When you're in a conversation, how often are you thinking what you'll say next?
- Do you already know the solution to the problem?
- Listen and be here now.

How to Get Out of Your Own Way: See It, Say It, Sort It

Giving Feedback—How It Works

Listening goes far beyond your natural hearing process. It means paying attention to the words that are being spoken with the intention of understanding the other person.

Use open questions starting with "when", "how", "what", and "who". Avoid questions starting with "why".

Say "Yes, and" instead of "Yes, but".

Do not use "always" and "never"; they disengage the dialogue.

Comment only on what you observe.

Keep feedback objective. Keep it simple.

When the other person is talking, keep quiet and listen. Offer no justification, no explanation, and no defence, even if you disagree.

Mirror and reflect back what has been said to you by paraphrasing. "What I'm hearing is" and "Sounds like you are saying" are great phrases to use to reflect back.

Enquire and ask open questions to clarify certain points.

Summarize the person's comments regularly.

See it. You observe something that you do not understand or recognize as suitable behaviour.

Say it. Do this always with kind intention and the aim to comprehend; ask open-ended questions.

Sort it. Together work towards a mutual understanding. Have a constructive dialogue.

Post-reflection. What worked? What didn't work?

Go to the journaling section on page 142.

Note any thoughts and opinions.

In what manner are you getting in your own way?

Chapter 8
Non, Je ne Regrette Rien

A woman with a voice is, by definition, a strong woman. But the search to find that voice can be remarkably difficult.

Melinda Gates

In 2013, I was asked by a group of professional bankers, all women, to give a talk about conflict management. I struggled. So much had already been said on this topic that I wondered what valuable information I could provide this audience who had given up their lunchtime to come and listen to me. I read up on and researched the topic and wanted to know for myself what conflict was. *Is it part of life? How do we deal with conflict?* I decided to call my talk "Kill the Voice and Find Your Own".

I shared my story and all the messages I had received from teachers and family members, mentioning that I was severely dyslexic and discussing how I accepted and carried the voices of the past with me wherever I went, particularly when it came to situations of conflict. I divulged to the audience that whenever I had to deal with conflict, I would exercise either fight (with my family) or flight (at work). So, my strategy was to shout or holler alone. I always used to say I was angry, but really, I wasn't angry. I was sad, hurt, and scared. But those feelings were not allowed in my world, because they make you weak and people take advantage of you when you are helpless. We all have a choice. However, when we are operating in our limbic system, we believe that we don't have any choices. This is when we go into "flight, fight, or freeze" mode, or we experience an amygdala hijack.

Goleman describes three signs of an amygdala hijack:

- strong emotional reaction
- sudden and intense emotional reaction
- saying or doing something or sending an email you later realize was inappropriate.

Goleman describes the amygdala hijack as an instantaneous and overpowering emotive response to stimulus which has activated major emotional danger. The amygdala is the part of the human brain that handles emotions. What is fascinating about the amygdala is that it does not depend on physical threats to be activated. But when it is activated, it causes us to become childish, as we have learned the behaviour we are now exhibiting in childhood. Indeed, the opposite of an amygdala hijack is emotional intelligence. It is crucial for us to stop in the moment so we do not get emotionally hijacked. People are always looking for quick tips, foolproof solutions, and foolproof strategies. I recognized this and thus articulated one of the best ways, in my experience, to manage conflict states, contexts, and interactions so as to become more aware. This is the true mechanism that is foolproof.

- Are stress and conflict, inner and outer, part of life?
- How do you deal with conflict?
- How can you prepare for conflict?

Indeed, awareness is the first step to generating what you want to truly understand in your life. When you focus on yourself, you will find that your responsiveness, your feelings, your responses, and your conduct determine how you manage conflict. Developing this awareness permits you to appreciate where your judgements and reactions are taking you. Take control of your emotions, behaviour, and personality so you can make the changes you want. Until you are mindful in the instant of your thoughts and emotions, you will struggle with resolving conflict and will not be able to focus on open dialogues.

My emotional needs weren't really met when I was young. I can see through my own work that past traumatic events and how we internalize them come back to disturb us if we do not deal with them. Part of coaching is to employ new strategies and thinking and to learn techniques that stick. One of the contexts where our wiring often needs repairing is in having a difficult conversation. We must learn to do this without shattering. This involves developing the ability to actively listen to the other person while neutralizing our emotions. It's about examining how we look at our interactions and discovering what is helpful and what is not.

An obligatory part of life, conflict is conveyed in countless ways. It intrudes into our everyday life, and if we are not prepared for it, it can be destructive and destabilizing. Learning about the amygdala made me realize that mine was on overdrive. If it perceives a threat, it can lead me to react irrationally and negatively.

Summary

- Ask questions.
- Know your triggers.
- Don't join the drama club.

Coaching Story: May

May came to me because she wanted someone to help her work on her communication style. At our first meeting, she sought support to explore specific issues that might be holding her back. What's more, she wanted to identify ways to unlearn some of the behaviours that she had developed. May's goal was to build on the specific issues that had come to the surface. Our first session was designed to establish goals and expectations for the coaching outcomes and to assess her current areas of strength and developmental opportunities.

May explained that she was ashamed by the number of times she had cried in meetings. The crying happened so fast that she couldn't seem to stop her reaction. Someone would say something, and in a heartbeat, she would be in tears. This is interesting as there is now so much information about the power of vulnerability. Exposing our weaknesses allows others to expose their own. In my experience, this can be risky and have repercussions at work. Hence, I would suggest sharing as much as you are comfortable with and have a sense of the context.

May asked me, "What is the fastest way to control the tears? Do you have any tips or strategies?"

I am often asked for tactics and tips. There is nothing wrong with this. Working through the issue at hand is slower, but slow and steady wins the race! Thus, I made it clear to May very early on that she would have to *do the work* and not expect a quick fix.

May told me that she was the only soft female amongst alpha males and alpha females. I asked her to give me some adjectives to describe an alpha female. She listed words like *loud, abrasive,* and *arrogant.* I asked, "Could it be that they are also *firm, courageous,* and *unapologetic*?" Then I asked how she would to describe herself. *Discreet, modest, humble.* We talked about whether her peers had these qualities too.

I heard many absolute statements from May. Absolute statements are statements such as "They will never change" and "He always screws up." Our brains receive these statements and ultimately deem them to be true and will even go further to hunt for evidence that confirms them as absolute.

"What beliefs about yourself do you need to let go of?" I probed.

"That being loud, abrasive, and arrogant is wrong."

I assured her that it was not about being wrong or right; it is about what happens to you when people around you exhibit these traits. Her response to crying was, in a way, enabling her to react but not to respond. The process of self-development requires a great deal of commitment, and addressing the specific targeted areas to take the necessary action for improvement requires deep exploration and self-reflection. I encouraged May to own her power, especially amongst those whom she perceived to hold power. As we fill our days with more and more "doing", I have noticed, going non-stop impedes our focus.

"No one," I assured her, "should have such power over you that you are not able to find your voice."

May agreed that indeed she tended to give up her power very easily and that crying was her way of trying to control situations and closing them down so the discomfort would stop. Once May recognized what was frustrating her and she fully understood her position, she began to take steps towards improving the situation. This was not only empowering; it ultimately led her to be more serene and more powerful.

How to Get Out of Your Own Way: Conflict Dialogue—How It Works

Before the dialogue, if you have time, write down the following responses:

- How can we do to better understand our differences and strengths?
- How can we leverage the communication?
- What are the obstacles for you and for the other?

During the dialogue, do these things:

- Breathe.
- Slow down to speed up; slow down your pace; lower your tone to speed up and get to the common purpose.
- Plan but don't script.
- Acknowledge your counterpart's perspective. Be considerate.
- Give something in return.
- Reflect and learn.

Go to the journaling section on page 144.

Note any thoughts and opinions.

In what manner are you getting in your own way?

Chapter 9
(Just Like) Starting Over

There is no limit to what we as women can accomplish.

Michelle Obama

When I was about fifteen years old, my mother would force me (yes, force me) to participate in Santoshi Mata *aarti puja* (prayer) with her. Santoshi Mata is honoured as the "Mother of Happiness", predominantly revered by women of India and Nepal. A ritual fast called the Santoshi Mata *vrata* and puja of sixteen successive Fridays earns the goddess's favour. Santoshi Mata was first revered in the 1960s by women in Uttar Pradesh. The *vratkatha*, or fast, on Fridays meant consuming only one meal throughout the day and offering *gur-chana* (raw sugar and roasted chickpeas, associated with the non-elite) as *prasad* to the goddess. When the devotee's wish is granted, he or she then organizes an *audyapan* (concluding ceremony), where eight boys should be served a festive meal. In contrast to Kali, who battles real demons, Santoshi Mata combats the everyday difficulties of her followers. She is the personification of the female life cycle and conveys the message that it is reasonable for a woman to expect her own satisfaction in the form of love, comfort, and respect.

While doing research for this book, I read that a low-budget Bollywood film made about Santoshi Mata in 1975 became one of the top blockbusters of all time.

I remember dreading these Friday prayers and sat begrudgingly, miming the words and reciting the prayers at a super-speedy pace so I could get back to watching television. The only appealing aspect was the fact that we would have gur-chana after the prayers had finished. Yet while I was doing reading and research for this book, I realized that Santoshi Mata is denoted as the goddess of contentment and that she acknowledges all the sorrows, all the problems, and the ill fate of all her followers and blesses them with success and pleasure.

As per the principles, she is a four-handed goddess, with only two hands evident to her devotees; the other two, which carry weapons, like a sword and *trishula* (a type of trident), are only for the people who place hurdles in the path of truth and goodness. So, there was a reason I learned about Santoshi Mata's devotions. I have a deep sense that Santoshi Mata has no malice or greed in her heart and believes in respecting every individual. Santoshi Mata is the symbol of love, gratification, compassion, contentment, and faith. She inspires an individual to cherish family values and to come out of crisis with determination.

I found it hard to understand how such a deep belief in one's faith could also create so much anxiety and fear. In Indian culture and others too, we give a lot of importance to *buri nazar* (the evil eye) and its hostile effects. In my family, my mother, a deeply religious person, was a hardcore believer in buri nazar. Consequently, in my own family, joy was always tinged and tarnished, and fear kept the buri nazar flame continuously lit. Indeed, if anything happened to her or the family, my mother would say that she was suffering from buri nazar.

Every time I said I was lucky, she would snap, "Chup kerr. Buri nazar lagna!" (Be quiet. The evil eye will get you!)

I never had full permission to embrace joy without the dark thought in the back of my mind that my joy would invite darkness, jealousy, and negativity.

An evil eye, it is said, can cause us to lose our aura and to feel drained and disempowered. My mother believed that some people possess the evil eye. Even though she had strong faith in God, buri nazar bothered her immensely.

In India, we hear a lot about *nazar lagna* and buri nazar. The evil eye is nothing but extreme negative feelings. In my experience, there is positive energy and negative energy. How we react to these two energies is our choice. For sure, these energies come in numerous forms, and we certainly know how we feel when we meet these two polar energies. But we have a choice. We can either be aware of what happens to us when we experience these energies, or we can criticize. In this respect, it is very important to get to know yourself, to understand your sanctity, and to feel comfortable with yourself, your actions, and your life.

At the same time, I was doing research for this book, I began looking into all the Indian goddesses, especially the ones I had grown up with and spurned. One of the deities who really struck a chord with me was Maa Durga. Maa Durga[11] is particularly celebrated in the north of India. I like to think of her as our Indian version of Wonder Woman. Her special superpower is kindness. The predominant incarnation of the primary energy named Shakti, Maa Durga is a manifestation of the Supreme Force and has the unique ability to take any form. Her intuition is greatly developed, and she uses it with great skill in her human relationships. She knows how to observe and listen to others; nevertheless, she is formidable.

Indeed, Maa Durga the Hindu goddess really impressed me as a child. Also called Divine Mother, she protects humanity from misery and evil by destroying the forces of evil such as prejudice, jealousy, ego, hatred, anger, and selfishness. When you show courage, that is Maa Durga's power in action!

Shiva is certainly one of the most important god, if not the most important god, of Hindu mythology. His hair flows in the Ganges,

---

[11] *Maa Durga* means "the inaccessible" or "the invincible".

which explains why this river is sacred in the eyes of Hindus. His main attribute is the trident called a trishula. This trident has a triple meaning: creation, perpetuation, and destruction.

We are all Durgas and Shivas in some form, all accountable for re-establishing balance when disparity is present. And, yes, we are, all of us, responsible for humanity. Wherever we live, we all want the best for the ones we love. We all want them to make the right choices. We all want to protect them and keep them from harm, whoever we are and wherever we are. We are all want to avoid suffering for ourselves and for the ones we love. We will all do our best to avoid suffering and have an enriched life. We are all affected by stress at some point in our lives. Stress is an inevitable part of life and a common cultural reality. Stress can represent different things to different people, but no one escapes it. It touches all of our lives, and how we deal with it is a personal matter, but this is a struggle we all face wherever we are. What is your dharma?[12]

Until recently, I had rejected my Hindu upbringing because I'd witnessed only a disconnect between prayer and action. However, I see that we are all divine beings and that the spiritual piece of our life prevails throughout. Dharma is the universal truth. In Hinduism, dharma is the right way of living, the moral order of the universe. No single English word effectively describes dharma. What I have come to understand about dharma from growing up as a Hindu is that it implies that we are all very small parts of a whole system, impacting each other for better or for worse.

---

[12] In Hinduism, dharma is the spiritual law for human beings. When people follow dharma, they feel good about themselves and find life to be most rewarding.

We all need love and recognition. No matter who you are or where you are, love is a feeling that you want to experience. Feeling loved validates us and helps us to feel important. Whenever you don't understand someone or feel detached from somebody, remind yourself that they, too, just like you, want to be loved and accepted. I have never met anyone who disagrees with this life truth.

We struggle to accept that we cannot control our lives 100 per cent of the time. Change is difficult to adapt to and accommodate. In this ever-changing world, coping with change is something we all endeavour to manage. The rapidity with which the world is changing now presents us with an omnipresent battle.

We all want to belong and feel part of a collective, to be included in a community. This is a need we all desire to fulfil. The path to inclusion requires modesty, openness, and kindness. We must simply be willing to learn to get along while recognizing our differences. This begins with a promise to adjust our behaviour to suit others.

What the world needs now is darshan. Meaning grace or a connection, darshan can ascend from a beautiful sunrise or a human connection, starting with a smile. The word *darshan* literally means attitude, perspective, and thinking. Consequently, by examining a person, one forms a belief about the person. One forms a judgement about the person. Heightened observation and awareness lead to improved understanding of that person. In Hinduism, darshan is considered a powerful form of worship and a process of spiritual fulfilment.

This form of respect does not need to be confined to a deity; it can be a simple glance, a gaze lasting a few seconds, saying to the other, "I see you, all of you." Darshan is a modest ritual. Simply observing is enough to bring about divine joy.

Summary

- What is your dharma?
- What strengths derived from Maa Durga or Shiva did you need in the past to succeed?
- What darshan can you offer?
- Why are you here on earth?
- What is your purpose?

Coaching Story: Claire

Claire was the head of a business line. When I saw her, she had been with the company for ten years, having started there as a graduate. She was later promoted and was in the thick of it when the company transformed from a small start-up to a major international organization. The CFO relied heavily on all the heads of business lines, especially Claire, as she was very successful in implementing new systems and processes.

Claire came back after a six-month maternity leave to find that things had changed a great deal at work. She started feeling uneasy in her role, and she began to feel increasingly isolated at work, excluded from get-togethers, meetings, and important decisions. This left her feeling unhappy and professionally snubbed, as she loved her job, her team, and her peers. Having a baby is both delightful and demanding and can bring even the fiercest woman to tears, not because we are weak but because we are human.

Coaching was offered to Claire by her line manager, who felt she needed support coming back to a new organizational structure and perhaps required a place to evaluate and review her own professional needs and objectives. When we started our session, Claire spent a lot of time explaining how her boss expected so much from her, how he relied on her, and how much pressure was on her to perform.

I asked her, "What expectations do you need to manage?"

Claire had extremely high expectations of herself. She felt a strong desire to be checked in and to be "on" all the time at work. Demonstrating to herself, her boss, and her team that nothing had changed was trying for her. Nevertheless, things had changed. She and her partner had had a baby, and there was no denying that both life and work would not be the same, for a while at least.

"My partner does not feel the same pressure. Both our lives have changed, and yet having a baby feels like a career badge for him and a career burden for me."

My question prompted her to think about how she needed to manage her own beliefs about women coming back after maternity leave. She had been so considerate with the women in her team, and yet for herself, she felt she had to carry on as usual. I reminded her that at times we forget to be kind to ourselves and that self-care is not selfish. It is actually the opposite. If we take care of ourselves, then we do not burden others with this chore and this charge. What really came through was that social beliefs of how women should behave are profoundly embedded and can have an enormous influence on our behaviour. I am glad to say that during our sessions, Claire put her Wonder Woman cape back into the cupboard. She is now much kinder to herself and, most importantly, more realistic about what she can do and what she can't.

How to Get Out of Your Own Way: The Past Does Not Equal the Future

To reframe something is to change its meaning by putting it in a different setting, context, or frame. The meaning of any event depends on how we frame it. When we change the structure, we change the significance and, with it, our responses and behaviours.

The basis of NLP (neurolinguistic programming), reframing using context, is the presupposition that every behaviour is useful in some situation. By thinking of a useful context, you can change your response to that behaviour. Putting a positive spin on ideas in politics is a typical use of reframing. Someone or some idea always sets the frame. Awareness of the meaning of the process gives us control over it. This is where the concept of words having power is at its most significant. What we use to describe something is an excellent example of reframing. For example, we may reframe a setback as an opportunity or a constraint as an advantage.

Before speaking, consider what you will say and in what way you will say it. The next time you meet a person, remember that words have power, so choose them wisely.

Go to the journaling section on page 146.

Note any thoughts and opinions.

In what manner are you getting in your own way?

CHAPTER 10
Stop to Love

Think of all the beauty still left around you and be happy.

Anne Frank

In January 2013, I was in London at my parents' home. It was six in the morning, and I woke up that morning with the whole right side of my body numb. I was very afraid, and while I knew I was under extreme stress, I never expected that it could have such a great impact on my body. At that time, I was juggling work, family, coursework for a master's degree, and frequent trips to London to care for my ailing mother. I had withdrawn from the world to concentrate on my mum and became consumed by her troubles. The climax inevitably came in January 2013. I woke up but could not get out of bed. I was washed out, kaput, completely defeated. I felt physically ruined. Never did I expect that the emotional stress would lead me to this physical state. In fact, this was not the first time I had experienced these symptoms. In 1999, I had felt the same numbness, symptoms of emotional and physical stress that I ignored.

So many times, the alarm bells went off, but I did not listen to any of them. I was wired and tired. I felt physically and emotionally drained and isolated, and the situation made me feel frustrated. I looked at myself in the mirror that morning, and I had real trouble recognizing myself. I experienced going through the motions, but I was not connected to my environment. It was like me watching a movie of myself. I started questioning the purpose of my role in life, and feelings of worthlessness and despair began to surface—manifested by me through irritation and tetchiness.

I had brain fog, my logical thinking and reasoning were strained, and I found it hard to think straight. The accumulation of stress, and my reluctance to use the resources available to me, resulted in a gradual depletion of energy and eventually chronic fatigue.

Managing stress in any form is difficult but not impossible, and therefore I believe one must devise fresh methods for dealing with stress at work. One must prepare for stress and self-manage stress to protect oneself from the unpleasant side effects. Improving self-stress management skills with the sole aim of achieving a healthy work-life balance is the goal. This, in turn, will have enormous positive benefits on your emotional and physical state, which are clearly interlinked. Be attentive to the resources and people available to you, both at work and at home, and use them. It's about knowing yourself, what you want, what you can handle, and what you don't want in your life.

With the current pace of life and increasing demands, there is no question that the brain is feeling a new and possibly damaging degree of pressure. Most people assume that this stress is simply part of life, but it really doesn't have to be that way. Work is part of life, and to be mindful of that is key, no matter where you are.

When you find ways of acknowledging your stressors once they appear, try to limit them by either avoiding them or dealing with them in another way and by employing the resources available to you. Prioritize, review your professional objectives, identify your stressors, deal with them (with the aforementioned tools) before they take over, and query your taxing thoughts.

In my work as a coach, I have seen a number of balanced, conscientious employees unexpectedly collapse, victims of burnout or depression. They crack because of the situations they are going through. They find themselves isolated sometimes by the people around them, who may remain silent, not knowing what to say or how to help. It is this silence from others that is extremely painful to bear. At work, the model of support starts from the top, and on a personal level as well a support structure needs to be in place.

One essential ingredient of emotional well-being is the exercise of gratitude. Expressing gratitude, being grateful, is a gift for our mind and, more astonishingly, for our body. Gratitude may be expressed in the moment, but it is also useful to cultivate it as a daily exercise, a habit you acquire. Keeping a journal of gratitude, where you record daily the kindness that warmed your heart, is easy to do and good for the soul. I endeavour to thank someone every day, as I am convinced that people need the warmth of someone along with their energy and their kindness. *Kindness* and *warmth* are not often words heard in the hard-headed business sphere, but they should be. Compassion and competence are vital elements for a successful business life.

To summarize, one needs to nourish the physical, emotional, mental, and spiritual parts of life. Go back and reflect to see what worked and when and why.

> - Think of yourself at this particular time or at a specific moment in the past when you felt most energized.
> - Think of yourself at this particular time or at a specific moment in the past when you felt most de-energized.
> - What are the differences? How were you operating? How many resources did you have?

We all have networks of people who can help us. This network extends from our professional and social lives to include our family, friends, and public services. Within your organization, your professional network includes relations with your boss, mentors within the organization, colleagues, your team, previous colleagues, and organizational support services. Outside your company, your network can include your friends, clubs, and social organizations. When you are experiencing acute stress, make sure you use these resources. Please don't try to do everything on your own.

The biggest difference in my life is that, unlike before, I am now more aware of the pre-alarm bells, and I now take care of my physical and emotional well-being. In times of self-doubt, I do an Amy Cuddy "power pose". I consciously put my shoulders up, stand in my power, breathe, and watch what happens inside me.

We all have stressful periods in our professional and personal lives, and we need the resources from work and from home to help us. For me, I think my exhaustion was due to an accumulation of stress and not purely confined to the imminent death of my mother. I made the fatal mistake of not resourcing myself and not doing the things I loved with the people I loved. We may not have the power to change the situation, but we do have the power to stop to love the people who care about us, to love our lives, and especially to love ourselves.

My boundaries may be different from yours, and what works for you may not work for me. Hence, listen to that inner voice. It always tells you the truth. Prioritize what is important, and let go of what is not. If you can't do the selection process yourself, then ask for help from a friend, manager, or coach. A state of mind is a subtle mix of emotions and thoughts; indeed, our moods are the heart of our inner life and our connection to the world. Always present, always influential, they accompany every moment of our existence. The French have a word: *profiter*. It means to take enjoy the moment, the present, the now.

Summary

- Personal life and professional life are not distinct from one another.
- If you discount your emotions, this will come back to bite you when you least expect it.
- Refuel yourself.
- Love yourself with all your heart.

Coaching Story: Sarah

Sarah requested to meet me in café and asked me several times if what we talked about would be completely confidential. I reassured her that all my work is private. We met in a café, and the first thing Sarah said to me before she sat down was "I am so sick of being judged by my looks. I thought it was supposed to be about my ability and skills, not how good-looking I am."

Certainly, Sarah was beautiful, and she was also authentic and personable. She wanted someone to challenge her, help her work through her goals, and guide her. We discussed the reality of judgement, being judged by how she looked and how she dressed. She confirmed that her looks had worked for her and had definitely opened doors for her. I felt for Sarah because it was difficult for her to determine whether someone liked her for who she was on the inside or how she appeared on the outside.

"How does that inhibit you?" I asked.

"I have become very conscious. I don't speak up too much. People just stare at me, making me feel extremely uncomfortable. The cruellest thing is that they love to assume that I'm shallow. I can't look like this and be smart. It doesn't pair."

Sarah's awareness of feeling dumb had come up several times in our sessions, and we explored how feeling dumb had affected her confidence. How had she unintentionally nourished this stereotype? Had she called it out? Had she told her colleagues how it made her feel? Taking ownership of what was happening around her meant she could then have some influence over the outcomes. We practised the "See it. Say it. Sort it" model with the intention of calling attention to certain undesirable behaviours or remarks made about her and the impact these had on her.

The result was positive for Sarah. Many of her peers had no idea how she felt, and she noticed a significant difference by speaking up. There was also another gift. By her speaking up, others in the team felt comfortable to speak up too about issues troubling them. Sarah paved the way for others to share their thoughts and opinions.

How to Get Out of Your Own Way

When you feel that you are completely overwhelmed and you lack the energy to do anything about it, the following tips can be helpful:

- Step back from the situation; take a day off from work, from school, from life.
- Focus on the important priorities and put them into action at once.
- Think about what you expect of yourself, what others expect of you, and what you have committed to fulfil.
- Talk about how you feel to someone you trust, and listen to their response.
- Give yourself positive feedback as you succeed in achieving your revised goals.
- Listen to your body before you exceed your limits. Let it return to what feels normal for you.

Ask your yourself and write down which areas need nourishment:

- Emotional?
- Spiritual?
- Physical?

Go to the journaling section on page 148.

Note any thoughts and opinions.

In what manner are you getting in your own way?

CHAPTER 11
I Feel for You

> People will forget what you said, people will forget
> what you did, but people will never forget how you
> made them feel.
>
> Maya Angelou

A lot has been said about the importance of kindness. But how do we instil these values in our society, institutions, organizations, and schools? How do we communicate this message, and where does the "be kind to others" crusade begin?

It doesn't matter whether we are talking about being kind to ourselves or others. Only when we learn to let go of the judgemental aspect of our minds, when we embrace forgiveness, when we acknowledge our shared human experience, and when we practise kindness do we discover true peace of mind and happiness in our lives. In relationships, it happens as we become more patient, better at listening, and perhaps a little kinder too. The range of benefits is vast and varies from person to person, but at the very least, being kind will make for a calmer and clearer mind.

> Kindness is at the heart of our humanity: giving, receiving, giving back. We are intertwined by these exchanges, some of which transform our lives in the long term.

In my interview with Andy Puddicombe, co-founder of Headspace, he reminds us to be kind. Whether we are talking in terms of being kind to ourselves or others, only when we learn to let go the judgemental aspect of mind, when we embrace forgiveness, when we acknowledge our shared human experience, and when we practise kindness will we discover true peace of mind and happiness in our lives.

Furthermore, in a heart-warming article in the *Harvard Business Review*, Bill Taylor reminds us that small gestures can send big signals about who we are. He takes heed of the wise words of Jeff Bezos (founder and CEO of Amazon). In a lecture to Princeton students, he advocated, "It's harder (and more important) to be kind than clever." Mr Bezos clearly stated the lesson that kindness begins in childhood and we are undisputedly moulded and influenced by the adults around us. And if we are lucky enough to have kind-hearted role models, well, that's a real bonus in our future lives. How we treat others surely has a bearing on how we will treat the people they meet. Ultimately, we teach people how to treat us.

One infallible method I have seen used to be successful and compassionate is to mirror behaviour to increase rapport. When we mirror the behaviour of those we wish to connect with, it is essential to mirror posture, gestures, facial expressions, and even breathing. To succeed and create a natural communication, we need to combine verbal and non-verbal characteristics. So be patient with people. Be kind to people. That's it. Be patient and be kind. Be empathetic.

Be curious. Curiosity (derived from the Latin word *cura*, meaning "care") is about learning, exploration, and investigation, and there is so much to be gained by being curious. Ask questions, discover more, and have a thirst for knowledge and your setting. Always ask open-ended questions—and wait for the other person's answers.

Be empathetic. Empathy helps to reduce social distance. We all need to foster this to make sure we build "deliberate moments" into our daily practice. A genuine understanding of others leads to improved bonds. And to be compassionate means having a true desire to help others and relieve stress.

Be interested. Be respectful and tolerant, reacting honestly with integrity and kindness. Choose to connect and develop a sincere interest.

Be patient. Don't be afraid of silence. It is a powerful tool and shows that you're listening.

Be the mirror. Adapting, modifying, and matching communication styles helps to build rapport.

Be humble. Overconfidence can hamper you unless you stop to question and practise humility.

Be the change you want to see. Put your empathy cards on the table and demonstrate to others that you do care and you do understand. Recognition and understanding are the keys to stronger relationships and sound interactions in a business context.

Summary

- Kindness is not a soft skill.
- When people know you care, they will care too.
- If you are going to talk the talk, you've got to walk the walk.

Coaching Story: Karen

Karen was a very successful professional. She was the CEO of a medium-sized company and described herself as emotionally intelligent with the ability to read people very well. Karen requested coaching because she wanted to know how she came across. Through my work with leaders, I know that feedback is like a birthday: it comes once a year and is often sugar-coated. Karen felt she knew herself and wanted endorsement and challenge when necessary.

When I met Karen, she had that killer combo I often talk about and rarely see—competency and compassion. We talked about her rise, or climb, to becoming the CEO, and I picked up phrases like "I got lucky" and "I was in the right place at the right time."

Granted, luck has a role to play in success, but it can only be part of the sum. Even though by her own admission she had made it, she was incapable of jettisoning the feeling that at any moment she would be found out and exposed as unsuited to the role.

"I have worked in this industry for twenty years. I know my stuff. Yet as soon as I mention I am the CEO, I feel the pressure to step up."

I very much appreciated her vulnerability in sharing, and I reassured her that she was not alone and that it was what she did with this heaviness that was the important thing. In my mind, although many women and minorities suffer from impostor syndrome, it is not just limited to in- or out-group behaviour. For me, feeling like an impostor is about confusing self-assurance for skill. People who tend to suffer from impostor syndrome[13] have low self-esteem despite their accomplishments. Women, minorities, and individuals of LGBTQ persuasion are more likely to suffer from impostor syndrome because of messages they received growing up in the family, at school, and in society. However, the reason you feel like an impostor is because you are unable to authorize yourself and give yourself consent that you do belong and you have a seat at the table.

---

[13] *Impostor syndrome* was coined in 1978 by clinical psychologists Dr Pauline R. Clance and Suzanne A. Imes. It refers to the condition experienced by high-achieving individuals marked by an inability to recognize their accomplishments and a consistent fear of being found out or exposed as a "fraud".

I asked Karen during one of our sessions, "How do you challenge yourself to give your power away?"

I saw that Karen was unable to assume responsibility for her successes, even though others admired her for what she had achieved. She acknowledged that she attributed her achievements to tremendous luck, which meant that she was holding on to old self-limiting beliefs. The first step was to recognize these impostor feelings when they arose. Only then could she begin to regain control.

Conscious that Karen put a lot of pressure on herself, I encouraged her to go easy on herself. If she did not succeed the first time, she should take the stumble as a starting point to improve for the next time, because there is always a next time.

How to Get Out of Your Own Way

What is your definition of kindness?
What kind act can you perform today?
What is the impact of your kindness on others?
What is the impact of your kindness on you?
How can your act of kindness create a ripple effect?

Go to the journaling section on page 150.

Note any thoughts and opinions.

In what manner are you getting in your own way?

CHAPTER 12
I'm Coming Out

> I have no time for women who don't support other
> women.
>
> Victoria Beckham

So much has been documented about women and leadership. You cannot avoid reading about cracking the code, shattering the glass ceiling, joining the top table, etc. Both on an economic and a social level, a great deal of research confirms the benefits of greater female inclusion at all levels of an organization. This is not just for true for productivity but also for equality and stability. As women, how gender will influence our perceived capability and ability is based on the *other's* experience.

Certainly, there has been a shift in the last few years. Women are starting to be seen as viable contenders, and I say *starting* because there is still a lot of progress to be made, not just in organizations but also in school and at home. Women's ability to cultivate competencies, such as collaboration and empathy, as a means of authority is an essential leadership quality needed for today's climate. And leadership is something we all do every day. It is about our collaborations with others, our aptitude to encourage others and to guide others to a common goal.

When I began working with both organizations and individuals,

I was coaching leaders to take their style of coaching into their leadership style. I noticed very early on in my career that coaching women was different and that, indeed, our society is still deeply filled with masculine archaism in its culture and structures. I was stunned when I heard women's stories of struggle holding key positions in top management despite having equal experience. When I listened to their stories of having to be better and of being treated differently because they are women, I was taken back to my own story of difference and gender.

I lived in a context where men had power. They had authority, right, and might. I was reminded that women did not have the same place as men and that our role was to serve our fathers, our brothers, and then our husbands. I remember when I was about fourteen seeing my mother preparing my younger brother's breakfast and adding a whole raw egg to his milk so that he would grow strong and tall. When I asked, "Where is my egg?" I was told I didn't need one because I was a girl. This is a frivolous example, and yet things like this have a continuing impact. I saw that being a woman and being a man had a different connotation, and consequently we were given different importance.

"Shine, but not too much" was the core message I received, and it was only when I started working and coaching my strong female clients that I realized this was a communal concept they had battled against as well. Their stories of being treated differently from their brothers, of men having enormous power in their families, was a situation I was also very familiar with. But these women were not Indian; they were Swiss, Irish, Brazilian, French, German, American, Italian, and Chinese.

Remarkably, when we shared, despite living across the globe, we found that we had all learned similar coping skills when it came to protecting ourselves. As I went through life, I realized how deeply I had internalized these self-limiting beliefs, that I was not good enough and not to sparkle too brightly, that I was neither respectable nor appropriate for a girl.

Curiously, by the time I had finished my studies, gotten married, and began working in London, and later on in Geneva, I recognized that gender preconceptions were not solely confined to my community and that I, like other "pushy" women, was being labelled as a go-getter and, dare I say it, ambitious. However, these traits were not perceived as positive attributes; rather, it was a mishmash rehash of the long-standing story for women across the globe. Women shared with me that being vocal and challenging was considered brusque, hostile, and rude. There were clear common costs that they all felt they were being made to pay as a result of being high-powered and daring to speak their minds. This was in 1992 and in 2018 alike.

Indeed, when I became a mother myself, my own mother reminded me of the importance of women, this time the importance of contributing to the family fund, and said that this was more important than any career development. As long as I was adding to my husband's account, I was proving my worth. I was blameless. It was contradictory advice, but all the same, the underlying message was "Women are subordinates, helpers, and assistants to the true deciders, men."

Luckily for me, I had taken Sheryl Sandberg's advice unknowingly in 1991 and married someone who has been the most important influence and supporter in my life and in my career.

However, I understand my mother's belief about her role as a woman and the role of women at work and in society in general. How could she have known any better? She had an arranged marriage at the tender age of seventeen, left all her family, and moved from India to London in the 1950s not speaking a word of English. Her journey was cruel; there were no female role models and no time to talk of empowerment or women's emancipation, and yet she did exceptionally well, unwittingly outshining her peers and her husband numerous times but not ever once acknowledging her own achievements herself. And if I am to be honest, as I endeavour to be in this book, I have to tell you that even today, in my fifties, it still hurts that I was never truly wanted. Yet this has given me a deeper empathy for how people, both personally and professionally, need to feel included and integrated. Moreover, I learned that resilience is an overwhelming quality that allows some people to be knocked down by life and come back stronger than ever. Rather than letting failure overcome them and drain their resolve, they find a way to rise from the ashes.

> Choice is about the opportunity and authority to decide. It is individual, it is personal, and it is something we need to support each other with.

I find it difficult to grasp that some women of my mother's generation still judge other women and determine what is right or wrong for us. They seem to be the arbiters of whether women should work after having children or whether women can have it all, and if so, how the bloody hell does she do it?

These are the real challenges. Women need to encourage women whatever they decide. That means if you decide to stay at home and look after your kids, you are no more or less than the women who decide to pursue their careers wholeheartedly. We all make different choices, and we as women need to respect each other's choices. As Madeleine Albright so rightly said, "There is a special place in hell for women who don't help other women."

I believe the media is largely to blame for preserving an image of women that is awfully redundant. The media still depicts women as followers and focuses less on their successes and achievements. Women who are achieving incredible things are still getting very little exposure. We still lack strong successful female role models in business, sports, medicine—in all areas. So here is the work for us all, to focus on the real issues and show up and stand for excellent female role models. We are all unsung heroines and need to raise consciousness of women's achievements.

And there are those women who choose to stay at home, as I did for a while during my career. This is the group I am anxious about because the work of the women who stay at home has never been counted. We all look at these women very differently.

Irrespective of our differences, we all have central human needs and emotions. It is vital and valuable to acknowledge our differences. In my work, I help my clients accept differences. As a female coach from a minority background, I believe that the conversation about difference needs to be opened and developed to create deeper authentic relationships. The uncertainty around how to handle diversity stems from the lack of knowledge, exposure, and training.

Having worked all around the world doesn't come without its challenges, and even though I believe I am open-minded, inclusive, and bias-free, I am human. Thus, when I began delivering the diversity and inclusion workshops, I felt it only right to examine my own unconscious bias and dig deeper to discover how my unconscious bias was affecting my own behaviour. Blind spots and biases impact our awareness of ourselves. Anytime a trait is hard for us to see, it is one we need to explore.

It was the revelation for me when I took the Implicit Association Test (IAT). The IAT was developed by Mahzarin R. Banaji. Banaji, a professor of psychology at Harvard University and co-author of *Blindspot*, along with Anthony Greenwald and Brian Nosek, created the test to help people recognize unconscious bias, and now this test is being used by companies to help employees understand that hidden biases are real. The simple battery of tests can be taken in approximately ten minutes and can be modified to assess unconscious bias in different categories, for example whether white test-takers are likelier to associate "good" words with white faces more quickly than with black faces. (They are, and black test-takers show the reverse results.) The IAT isn't meant to embarrass people; rather, it asks what steps we could take to improve the situation. When I took the IAT online, I was astonished by my results. Here I am an Indian woman, teaching, living, and breathing diversity and inclusion, and yet I found I had an implicit bias about women! I realized I have a bias, and none of us are exempt.

When I was growing up, men and women had different roles. Men in my family had power and thus authority. In my childhood home, men's voices were more significant than women's, and this stayed with me unconsciously until it showed up in my IAT results. One thing for certain is that these types of experiences act as collective filters when we make assessments and judgements of people around us. Besides this, research tells us that human beings have a natural tendency to place individuals into social classifications, and these groupings are often based on visual cues such as gender, cultural background, age, height, and body size. We also catalogue people based on their social background, professional roles, religious distinctiveness, and political affiliation. In my experience, the entire unconscious bias debate drives connection, whereas I have seen in the past that racist discussions generate disconnection.

When it comes to gender bias, one thing is certain: it's hardwired into us. And sometimes, as women, this means we are biased against ourselves, believing the stereotypes we hear. Agreed, it is not intentional, and thus the unconscious people preferences we make that are formed in childhood, through our education, are often a mishmash of all our experiences that come together to form our predispositions and preferences. For a long time, psychologists and researchers have been tormented about the particular question of how we get to know what is really going on inside the mind of a person. People do not consciously want to be biased but may not be aware that they are. But if we keep seeing males in positions of authority or power, something gets triggered to the unconscious brain, and thus we will continue to be biased unless we start seeing females in positions of authority and power.

If all your life you've been exposed to messages, consciously and unconsciously, that white skin is beautiful, you will unconsciously make these associations, and these will impact your decision-making and your choices, but if you become aware of it, you can slow down the process. When people do not believe that they have a scrap of preference, uprooting the bias becomes very difficult to tackle. We do, we all do, and we are all too quick to categorize people instead of identifying what skills people bring to the table. Unconscious bias often surfaces when we're multitasking or when we're stressed, as research shows. It comes up in tense situations when we don't have time to think and we try to make snap decisions. It's part of our evolutionary fight-or-flight response. It's automatic. We all have stereotypes that we are not aware of. That doesn't make us bad people. However, becoming aware of unconscious bias but then ignoring how it shows up in our daily life is bad practice. The challenge is to be realistic and not to pretend to eliminate biases but to try to interrupt them so we can behave in ways that are aligned with our values.

Working against the odds is hard enough, but one thing we need to do as women is to lift each other up and not criticize each other. That is the only way we are going to advance. When someone has your back, believes in you, and provides a safe place for you to thrive, who knows what you can do? Women are the future. We must not separate but celebrate each other. Find a female mentor, a female supporter, and absorb all the power and knowledge she can give you. There is plenty of room for us; we just need to take our space.

I have been very fortunate in my career. I've had many female allies who carried me when I thought I would fall. They saw a talent in me before I saw it, and these women aspired to be as great as men and lead high-level organizations. They were confronted with particular struggles with authority, and this went way back. I learned that everyone needs to be responsible for facilitating changes in attitude and behaviour. In organizations, a leader's role is to develop their people, their talent, and their potential. And, please, you do not have to be head of a team or a department to be a leader. We lead families, groups, neighbourhoods, and of course ourselves.

Women have a fear of letting down their guard and showing their vulnerability and compassion; it is perceived as being too dangerous. And I have seen that compassion and competence is a killer combination! The challenging part is to make ourselves visible, daring to celebrate our achievements by promoting ourselves. I, through my own journey, help women to stand in their power, and the only way we women can do this is to know ourselves.

In my view, women need to put themselves forward. I have often found myself, when given a new opportunity or having been chosen for a project, asking myself, "Am I good enough?"

I remember once when I was chosen out of a group of highly esteemed coaches to run a diversity and inclusion workshop for an organization. One of my friends said to me, "I bet you got that job because you are really good at what you do."

So deep was my self-doubt that my immediate reply to her was "I think I got it because I am Indian and I'm a woman."

"What? That is not walking the talk! Stop that now! Would you ever hear a man say that? You're listening to the wrong voice."

Lesson learned. Think before you speak. Words have power, and when in self-doubt, say nothing.

There are times when I have thought that I did not get a job because of my gender and colour, and I have come to realize that maybe I have personalized negative things that have happened to me without taking full responsibility for whatever problem has come my way. It's called the blame game!

Yet when I have depersonalized the experience and stood back, taking ownership of the problem, I was able to see that it could have been my gender and colour, or it could have been something else. We certainly do need more self-belief, and that does not mean being arrogant but promoting ourselves in a way that makes us appeal to others.

I think we have to be realistic because we now live in a culture that has tremendously high expectations. We strive for perfectionism, and the simple truth is that life isn't a smooth ride. However, having a support network of people you can trust is fundamental. You don't have to share everything. Hold your boundaries; listen and learn; and share and care.

We are still developing from a mainly male-controlled world. I have seen in my coaching practice and in my life that the opinions of female leaders have created a series of biases which start at birth, continue at school, and so on. When I coach women, we look at how and why they have taken on certain behaviours. These behaviours could have been either adopted by accident or inherited from primary caretakers or authority figures. Why we continue to play them out and how is always worth exploring. Subsequently, in my sessions, we play out those worst-case scenarios and challenge the truth of fear-based thoughts.

I have worked with some really incredible women who are powerful, kind, and strong. In fact, I observe that they all share that killer combo: compassion and competency! Watch out; it is potent!

I always start my sessions with three questions:

1. Where would you like to be?
2. What might be getting in your way?
3. What outcomes are you hoping to see?

My objective is to encourage my clients to self-reflect, and therefore it is crucial to be able to create a safe and non-judgemental environment, encouraging open and honest reflection to enable personal growth. When people are given the time and space to reflect and learn something new about themselves and others, the result is gold. With all the courses I have delivered for women, I have noticed one thing that is really powerful when women support women: we can do incredible things. So, I invite you all to open the door wide for each other.

My questions are similar for men too, but I have found in my work that it is often women who worry about being good enough and ready for the challenge or the promotion, and many doubt whether they can do it.

Summary

- Be adaptable towards each other.
- Be accepting of each other.
- Together we are better.

Coaching Story: Malika

Malika worked in the health domain. She was a unit manager and came to me because of some issues at work. Malika was a Muslim. She wore a hijab and was the only Muslim and only woman to be in an executive position in the organization. She had recently been promoted and gone through the hiring process effortlessly. She was recognized by top management not only as someone who was marvellous at her job but also as someone who was a leader and who had high potential for the group.

However, despite her credentials and reputation, when Malika came to me for our first session, she was unhappy with the remarks and comments about her race, her religion, and the rivalry she felt amongst her peers.

"Do you know what is like to be treated as the token Muslim member of your team?"

I did not know what it was like for Malika, so I asked her, "Tell me what it is like to be treated as the token Muslim member of your team?"

"I am constantly asked for comments about incidents in the news relating to anything Muslim. I feel as if I am the spokesperson for the whole Islamic world. When we have a team meeting, it feels like I am the target. It's hard to manage, but I do manage."

"How do you manage?" I asked Malika, sensing she was becoming emotional as she spoke.

"I am polite and answer as best I can, but I don't feel like I am qualified to talk about the whole of the Muslim community. It rarely has anything to do with what we are talking about in the meeting."

I could see Malika was offended, and together we looked at ways to manage the situation.

"I can't push back, because then I look as if I am taking things personally and making it about me. Plus, it will be uncomfortable for all of us. Surely you understand that."

And I did understand, because Malika was spot on. There are many comments I have witnessed, and I chose to minimize them. I chose comfort over awkwardness, harmony over discord. Consequently, I did something in my session with Malika that I don't do often: I divulged some information about myself.

I recounted a situation that happened to me during a workshop I was delivering. A company asked me to deliver diversity and inclusion training for their team. I rolled up on the day fully engaged, encouraging the participants to take responsibility when they saw, heard, or witnessed any discrimination or bias. I explained to the group that when I am with groups of people, I also notice exclusion, and said that we are all responsible, both part of the problem and part of the solution. I went on to describe to the group a real-life thing that happened to me in which I saw a strong gender bias with a client I was working with. After I finished the story, one of the participants put up his hand to raise a question.

"Yes, go ahead," I said.

"Did you say anything to this client when you saw that he was being biased?"

I stopped and waited for a moment, and I thought, *How do I answer the question? Do I choose honesty over dishonesty?*

"Nope," I said, feeling quite exposed, "and you have taught me something today, namely that there is absolutely no use in me urging people to stand up and speak up when I am not able to do it myself." Since that day, when I hear bias—about race, religion, gender—or see any discriminatory behaviour I say something, because if I don't, then I am part of the problem.

Malika seemed somewhat appreciative of my admission. There was something about pretending that by not saying or acting on the problem, it would somehow go away.

How could Malika say something that would leave her feeling less resentful later?

I suggested that whatever the remark was, it was essential to manage her mental state as she needed to model appropriate behaviour. The crucial piece is *how* to confront the behaviour. There is no one method. Yet I recommended that she react swiftly, tell the person how he or she made her feel, and also treat the person who made the remark with respect.

So that is what she did. She told me that when she stood up after having done what I'd suggested, her legs felt like jelly and she was hot and sweaty. And the need to call it out was met with appreciation. Afterward, people in Malika's team were more mindful about what they said to her. For Malika, it was the beginning of a new pattern of behaviour: "nipping it the bud".[14]

---

[14] "Nip in the bud" is a gardening term. Used figuratively, the expression usually means to prevent a potential problem before it advances.

How to Get Out of Your Own Way

What messages did you receive about women when you were growing up?

What messages did you receive about leadership when you were growing up?

What messages did you receive about women at school and later on?

Were you encouraged to speak up and share your ideas and opinions in your family?

Were you encouraged to speak up and share your ideas and opinions at school and later on?

What impact does that have on you today in your family, with your friends, and at work?

Go to the journaling section on page 152.

Note any thoughts and opinions.

In what manner are you getting in your own way?

Chapter 13
This Must Be the Place

> My father was an absolutely wonderful human being.
> From him, I learned to always assume positive intent.
> Whatever anybody says or does, assume positive
> intent.
>
> Indra Nooyi

Life is not crammed with smooth lines. It goes up and down like the sea. And like the sea, we appear rather calm, although beneath the surface, hidden from the eye, there's all this commotion. And it's a good cue to remind ourselves that we are all human and we are all on this voyage and never really get to the end. And today, when the thunderstorms come, I know you can endure this, because you have the awareness, the confidence, and the strategies to cope, and you know how to get out of your own way.

As I have seen in my life, many people have a vision and great ideas, yet very few see them through. This is because when we transform, not everyone will like it, and the fear of disapproval can easily fill us with unease and anxiety. It's all part of our human state to have feelings of discomfort and apprehension when we make changes. And it is all right. Some people will not approve of your choices, and it is not your job to make them approve. Stop trying to be everything to everyone today! This is your time to liberate and transform. Let your heart guide you, and follow your truth.

Be conscious of the people who love you, aware of things that trigger you, and alert to the things that make you better, and know that you are good enough. You are now standing *with* yourself and not *in front of* yourself, not getting in your own way. Listen to your inner voice. It's saying, *Stand in your power.* Step into your power, and stop wasting time saying no to your dreams. Say yes to the transformation that awaits you! What are you waiting for? Get out there and do what needs to be done, and get out of your own way.

> *Moksha* (nirvana, enlightenment) is now. Dispersed through moments and sprinkled in all our lives, it is not a permanent state. That is not feasible. Just enjoy these moments and *profite* while and when you can. Life is not a dress rehearsal. Live it, all of it.

Without hope, we would not brave the danger. Hope is what makes us go forward, dream, live, and believe again. Without hope, no change can be made towards a better life. Hope makes us look towards a better tomorrow.

Remember that when we are authentic, others can be too. And when each of us makes these micro-changes in our behaviour, in our actions, the amalgamation of these micro-transferences has a great impact on our families, our society, and our organizations.

No one makes it alone. We are all in this together. We learn from each other and help each other along the path. We can't really do too much deprived of one another. When I care about you, you care about me, and we care about each other. This has a ripple effect in the team and in the organization. Find your tribe and make a difference! There are millions of unsung heroines out there, so please, let's support all our sisters, friends, and colleagues. Locally, globally, remotely— wherever they are, let's help them find their voices too. And as we become more whole, we affect others as we take that into the world. Successful women shine from within, and then they radiate that warmth outwards, above, and beyond.

My whole life ethic is based on this Maya Angelou quote: "People will forget what you said, people will forget what you did, but people will never forget how you made them feel."

This is something that I respect and remember every day. Thus, what I consider to be the main success is to provide darshan for people so that they feel safe and empowered. This has a ripple effect and creates a deeper self-awareness and, in turn, a shared compassion in our global community. Life is a process. Every part of it is moving. Nothing is ever completely still.

Summary

The beauty of unlimited possibility is inside all of us.

Coaching Story: Lina

Lina had come to me via a recommendation from her CEO to participate in a coaching program. I asked her why she sought coaching.

"I feel a bit lost. I want to do something that excites me. I need a new purpose. I am not unhappy. I have a great job, a great family, and a great life. I know I am lucky, but I don't have a clear vision of what I want to become. It might sound ridiculous, as I am forty-seven, but I still have a whole lot of life ahead of me. There are things I want to do professionally, and I feel I am being boxed in. And no one else is doing it. It's me. I know I have a choice. I just don't know what it is."

Indeed, finding meaning in work affects our happiness and that of those around us, and work gets harder when it starts to lose meaning.

Besides this, the expectations of what our lives and careers should look like can cause us agony. We are often focused on what is missing, what we don't have. Hence, I suggest a gratitude exercise. The whole concept of developing an "attitude to gratitude" can sound very indulgent; however, it is these moments, when we chronicle what we are grateful for, that help us feel calmer and more thankful.

We discussed the gratitude exercise, and Lina agreed to do. She came back a few weeks later with a small purple notebook. She had kept it close to her for the last three weeks. As she opened it, I saw many scribbles and notes jotted down.

Lina smiled as she explained, "I have this with me all the time now. I know we discussed writing down what I am grateful for at night, but I keep this with me constantly. I take it to meetings, dinner with family, and drinks with friends. I write down what I am grateful for and when my energy is high, as we discussed. People think I'm nuts, but it has given me so many insights."

"What type of insights?" I asked.

"I notice that most of my gratitude notes involve times when I am with people. I love interacting with people. I get energy from seeing people, developing people, coaching people, and helping them to achieve their goals."

"Great. So you were able to jot down what you were grateful for in the moment? I think it is significant that you said, 'I get energy from seeing people develop.' How much time do you spend with people?"

"Not as much as I would like to—and that is something I have really learned about myself. I have actually discussed it with Pete [her CEO], and we are going to look at a role or a project together where I have more interface with people."

"It's very positive that you shared this with your boss. I believe that we all recognize energy but aren't consciously aware of it. Identifying what gives us energy means paying attention, and that is how the journaling exercise helped you. Let's do another exercise, OK?"

"Sure," said Lina.

"Picture your life in ten years' time. Reflect on what you have done. Were you able to achieve what you set out to do? Did you become a better version of yourself? What inspires you about this person?"

Lina reflected. "If I hold myself accountable and make sure I am responsible, then I see someone who is contented, who led a life that was true to her. She spent the second part of her career developing others so they could rise."

"What inspires you about this person?" I enquired.

"That she lived a life that was true to her, with no regrets."

"Now here comes the hard part, Lina. What do you need to do daily, weekly, and monthly to get to this place?"

"It's not rocket science. I guess I need to create a practical timetable on a daily, weekly, monthly, and yearly basis."

"Whom would you need to involve to keep you accountable?"

She smiled. "You."

"Agreed," I replied, "and only for a month. I can see that if you stick with this routine for at least a month, it's very likely to become a habit, part of your routine."

How to Get Out of Your Own Way

- Accept the emotions that arise—good, bad, and ugly.
- Know that you are good enough.
- Be yourself unreservedly.
- Love yourself with all your heart.
- Give yourself permission to be human.
- Allow yourself to feel how you feel.

The irony is that only when we accept our feelings do we offer ourselves permission to be human and experience painful emotions. Consequently, we are more likely to open ourselves up to positive emotions.

Every new day brings a fresh chance to try again. Therefore, do not get discouraged. The past is gone, and tomorrow is another day.

Go to the journaling section on page 154.

Note any thoughts and opinions.

In what manner are you getting in your own way?

Chapter 14
Gaata Rahe Mera Dil

> Everyone needs to be valued. Everyone has the potential to give something back.
>
> Princess Diana

There was no mention of more sex or bungee jumps when a palliative nurse, Bronnie Ware, counselled patients in their final twelve weeks, recording their last wishes. Ware, who supported the dying in their last days, has revealed the most common regrets we have at the end of our lives in her book *Top Five Regrets of the Dying*. Bronnie is convinced from her work that if we cannot develop compassion for ourselves, we are going to have regrets.

The top five regrets of the dying, as witnessed by Ware, are these:

"I wish I'd had the courage to live a life true to myself, not the life others expected of me."

"I wish I hadn't worked so hard."

"I wish I'd had the courage to express my feelings."

"I wish I had stayed in touch with my friends."

"I wish that I had let myself be happier."

Most people will have some regrets. We all have a purpose that we came here to carry out. Yet most of us do not allow ourselves to heed to these internal dogmas. We only have one shot at life, and so we had better make the best of it. I often ask clients, "What are your favourite things in life? What inspires you? Which activities or people do you enjoy? What gives you energy and makes you happy?" Once they provide the answers, I encourage them to pencil in time for these activities despite their busy schedules.

I always pass the following intimate story on to my clients, and I would like to pass it on to you. It was profound for me and changed how I perceive life, my relationships, and my work.

I once knew a woman who had grown up in a very poor family in India. When she was seventeen, she had an arranged marriage and subsequently moved to England with her husband. To earn money, she had to work in a factory. She prayed and prayed for an office job, telling God that after she got one, she would be happy. Her prayers were answered—she got an office job—but still she was not happy. She lived with her husband in a rented flat. She prayed and prayed for her very own house and told God that after she got her own house, she would be happy. Her prayers were answered and she got her own house, but still she was not happy. She had two daughters, and during her third pregnancy, she told God that if he gave her a boy, she would be happy. Her prayers were answered and she got a boy, but still she was not happy. She was not poor anymore, but she wanted to have enough money so she would feel financially secure in her old age. So, again she prayed and prayed, this time for more money, and told God that after she got the money, she would be happy. Her prayers were answered, and she came into a considerable amount of money, but still she was not happy.

In 2011, she was diagnosed with stage IV terminal lung cancer, and on 23 February 2013, I was in her hospital room with her. On a cold Saturday morning, from her hospital bed, she ushered me to come nearer to her. And with hardly any voice or energy left, she told me, "I want to die. I have had enough."

I sat silently, trying to absorb her decision.

Once I found my voice, I asked her, "What message do you have for us, the ones who will be left behind?"

She waited for a moment and then said with fortitude, "Be happy now. Don't wait for tomorrow."

The woman was my mother, Saroj Bala Thapar, Rani (meaning "Queen") as she was fondly known. She went into a coma eight hours after our conversation and died the next day, Sunday, 24 February 2013, on my youngest son's fourteenth birthday.

I suppose that she was unknowingly my first coachee, as I recall from the age of nine or ten my encouraging her to become her best and trying to help her to get out of her own way. However, she lived in a context that was incredibly harsh. She spent her life trying to make the best out of a tough situation. I just knew she could be greater. I could visualize much more for her than she could have possibly imagined.

Death was her ultimate wake-up call, and fatefully, it was only when my mother knew she was dying that she truly began to live her life, making me realize that pain is unavoidable but suffering is optional. Loss is a huge discloser. It forces us to think of our own mortality and the fear attached to it. For years, I craved for my mother to be her authentic self, but she rarely showed it. Paradoxically, it was only after she was diagnosed with terminal cancer that she finally learned how to get out of her own way and live her truth for eighteen months, until her death at seventy-four. My wish is that she has truly found peace at last.

I love my work and the clients and organizations I assist. For me, coaching is about love, empathy, and kindness. It is about the sense of compassion and concern for the other—no judgement, just pure watchfulness during the time we are together. It might not sound very business-like, but I know this practice is why I have been so successful. Moreover, my spirit is not to be confined to a coaching relationship. It also works with my friends, my connections, and my contemporaries. When we show that we care about people, in whatever small amount, the impact is huge! People feel seen and feel heard, and that is powerful. Honestly, it is not difficult, but it does take a mindful effort, something we may need to consider to do as a minimum every day. Making this a daily practice has helped me to see from the inside out, towards others and beyond.

Even though I feel professionally gratified, I wanted to do something polar opposite to my world of executive coaching. So now, in my free time, I am a volunteer at La Maison de Tara, a non-profit, secular foundation in Geneva, Switzerland. La Maison de Tara is a hospice that offers an alternative to hospitalization for people nearing the end of life who are unable to stay at home but wish to spend their final days in a non-medicalized atmosphere surrounded by warmth, care, and tenderness—a home away from home. How we die is a profoundly personal journey, and it is not easy to fully comprehend the practical things one may need to think about when caring for a dying person and, of course, how a death can affect family relationships. I am welcomed and trusted to be part of the family from the very start. People often ask me, "Isn't it depressing to work in a place where people die?" They could not be more wrong. The atmosphere is caring, loving, and sincerely sunny.

Increasingly in our society, many people do not have a family or social network that is sufficiently wide to offer a sense of community care. A sense of loss may generate very strong emotions, which may be difficult to cope with for the patient, the family, and close friends. At La Maison de Tara, the staff considers that the spiritual dimension is an integral part of a human being. This gives meaning to everything and takes on a profound, truly essential element when one's life is coming to an end. It is here that we are encouraged to accept people just as they are, with their bad moods, fears, and anger, but also with joy, love, and the whole of our humanity. The need to reconnect to our personal resources is paramount at this time.

My very first time volunteering at La Maison de Tara, I parked my car outside, prepared to put into practice all the wisdom and learning I had received from Anne-Marie Struijk (the founder of La Maison de Tara) and the trainers. One of the very last things my mother said to me in the hospital was, "You should do this work, care for the dying." And for a split second, as I turned my car off, I sat in the parking lot and wondered, *Does my mum know I am here?*

I walked into Tara to start my duties, and one of the members of the volunteering team asked me to inform Danielle, one of the residents, that lunch was ready. I knocked on Danielle's door and walked in. There was Danielle, sitting up in her bed, listening to music. I recognized the music immediately, a familiar sound from the past—it was a bhajan.[15] As I turned to Danielle to help her up, I saw on her bedside table a photo of Sai Baba,[16] the same guru my mother so staunchly believed in. I was stunned. Danielle caught my reaction and asked me if I knew him. I told her my mother was a great believer and said that I couldn't believe she was too.

Through our many discussions after that day, Danielle talked to me about her trust in Sai Baba—what he had brought her and how he had helped her face life and, now, death. She had attended Sai bhajans in Geneva regularly, but since her illness, she had not been able to go for over a year. I asked her if she wanted to go together to the sai bhajans and if I could drive her. She said yes straightaway. That wonderful Thursday afternoon, I felt very joyful. I went to collect Danielle, and we chatted all the way there and back. I listened

---

[15] *Bhajan* is a Sanskrit word meaning "singing to glorify God". It is the name used for a Hindu devotional song and hymn.

[16] Sai Baba was an Indian spiritual guru regarded by his devotees as a saint.

carefully to her every word, as this I knew this was our precious time. I will always remember Danielle's face when she arrived at the centre that day. She was treated like family—everyone hugging her and giving her love, blessings, and light. We sat together and sang together and chanted together. At times, I surreptitiously looked at her out of the corner of my eye and saw her beaming face and luminous smile. I grew close to Danielle, and she helped me enormously to accept that belief, religiosity, and spiritualism take many forms and have many expressions.

The last time I saw Danielle was in April 2018. Because of work commitments, I was unable to volunteer at La Maison de Tara for the whole month of May, so I signed up for the first available time slot after that, which was in June. I was excited to see Danielle. Two days before I was due to volunteer, I received an email from La Maison de Tara saying that Danielle had passed away. Life is a terminal condition, as she'd told me many times before, and I understood she was terminally ill, yet I was still shocked and shaken. When I arrived the next day to volunteer at Tara, the coordinator asked if anyone wanted to look after Danielle. I was puzzled. I thought she had passed away. She had, and her body had been laid to rest in her room at Tara so family and friends could come and pay their last respects. Our job was to make sure her bhajans were always playing softly in the background and to light incense in her room while the music was on. Therefore, when this opportunity arose, I jumped at the chance to be with her one last time.

I went into Danielle's room and was met by a vision. She was lying there in her beautiful golden salwar kameez,[17] holding her prized prayer beads, peaceful and serene.

I sat next to her on a chair and just looked at her for a while. I thought about our car ride and all the plans she had made when she was to leave La Maison de Tara. I thought about how she told me about her own family, her loving brother and her extraordinary mother.

---

[17] A type of suit with loose trousers and a long shirt. It is worn especially by women in India and Pakistan.

And I thought about how she would often tell me, sitting in her bed, looking weary and pale, "You see, Sunita, I am so lucky. I have always been surrounded by love and affection."

I thanked Danielle for all she had given me, all she had taught me, and all she had done for me. I kissed her goodbye and whispered, "Sairam."[18]

We only get one life, and to go forward in our lifetime, we all need to get out of our own way. I invite you to stare inwards. It's not about others; it's about you. Look back and note unworthy patterns. Explore formative relationships and their impact on you—your ideals and beliefs and how they may get in your way today. We all have hopes, dreams, and goals, and nobody wants to have a life that is disheartened. Once you become the master of your own self, no person and no circumstance can reduce you. It is your responsibility to assume accountability. When you truly believe this, when you fully consent that it is your duty to do the work, you will find the charioteer for your transformation, and subsequently you will be better, do better, and live life better.

We make choices all the time. Happiness is a choice, so don't wait for tomorrow. Be happy now.

How to Get Out of Your Own Way

- Practise, practise, practise to transform useless thoughts and patterns.
- Make yourself your ultimate case study.
- Be in the now.
- Look back, but don't get locked in the past.
- Know that the past and the future are states that hijack you and keep you from being present.
- Do something different; change your reactions.

---

[18] *Sairam* is a religious greeting linked with devotees of Sai Baba.

- Turn up and turn off the harmful inner babble.
- Focus on where you want to get to, and then do the work.
- Have clear boundaries.
- Surround yourself with people who want you to win.
- Remember to tell yourself you are in control.
- Be happy now.

Chapter 15
Every Day I Write the Book

> Journaling is a practical and accessible way to stay connected to your inner self, your body, your dreams and your purpose in life.
>
> Charles Duhigg

Do you ever seem all topsy-turvy and upside down? Taking a few minutes to jot down your thoughts and emotions will nippily get you in touch with your inner world.

I have kept a journal on and off for the last thirty-five years. Journaling is one the most successful development tools, if not the most successful developmental tool, I recommend to my clients. I believe that journaling is the most effective bedrock practice you can cultivate. It has helped me become more aware of my thoughts, my drivers, my behaviour, and my reactions. Plus, I periodically write down lessons learned and milestone moments passed so I have a reference, a record of what has happened and what worked so I may use it in the future.

Journaling has helped me do the following things:

- Illuminate my understanding and thoughts.
- Get to know myself better.
- Disentangle painful emotions.
- Understand the other's point of view and manage conflict.

In fact, so powerful is journaling that Maud Purcell, a psychotherapist, founder and executive director of the Life Solution Centre of Darien, and journaling expert, says, "Writing accesses our left hemisphere of the brain, which is analytical and rational, while our left brain is occupied, our right brain is free to do what it does best, i.e. create, intuit and feel. Hence journaling, writing removes mental blocks and allows us to use more of our brainpower to better understand ourselves and the world around us."

Without question, journaling has definitely been the top inspiration for everything I do. Journaling is a habit you can recommence at any time. You don't have to journal every day; even a few times a week is extremely valuable.

You do not need to make a massive commitment. Try it for ten days. I recommend spending five to ten minutes a day reflecting in your journal. When the ten days are up, return and review what you have absorbed and the growth you've made. Then you can decide if you want to continue journaling. I would also encourage you to carry your journal at all times and have it available to you during the day. Some people are very structured regarding when and where they journal. I would invite you just to make sure you choose a time when you will be uninterrupted from doing your journaling. Journaling helps us deepen our connection with ourselves and expands our self-awareness so we can better connect with others. I have noticed in my work that when clients write down and note their thoughts and feelings and record their emotions, their growth is more sustainable and enduring.

You may find that journaling also helps you to release some of your emotional responses to events that have happened throughout the day as a way of dealing with any stress. This can help you to process and perhaps may encourage you to explore more positive reframing options.

Remember, when you journal, bring your whole self to the process.

Personal Notes

My current challenge

_____

_____

_____

_____

_____

_____

My current constraints

_____

_____

_____

_____

_____

_____

My current resources

_____

_____

_____

_____

How am I getting in my own way?

Chapter 1: Forest Fire

What powerful positive statements will you carry today?

_____

_____

_____

_____

Which WEBs are keeping you stuck?

_____

_____

_____

What were you thinking? What were you feeling? What will you do differently now?

_____

_____

_____

How did you get out of your own way?

_____

_____

_____

How are you getting in your own way?

_____

_____

_____

_____

_____

_____

_____

_____

_____

_____

_____

_____

_____

_____

_____

_____

_____

_____

_____

_____

_____

_____

_____

Chapter 2: What Have I Done to Deserve This?

Silent—Get yourself into a quiet and still space, internally, physically, and emotionally.

Timeout—Impose a timeout on yourself, a momentary interruption of your activity. When will you do this?

Impact—What power does this person or context have over you?

Let go—Break the thinking of what someone else did or didn't do, and release.

_____

_____

_____

_____

_____

_____

_____

_____

_____

_____

_____

_____

_____

How to Get Out of Your Own Way

What is it that makes it worth it for you to consider changing?

If things worked out exactly the way you want, what would be different?

What are the pluses and minuses of changing and not changing?

If this change were easy, would you want to make it?

What makes it hard?

How are you getting in your own way?

_____

_____

_____

_____

_____

_____

_____

_____

_____

_____

_____

_____

_____

Chapter 3: Dancing in the Dark

When you sense a challenging reaction, the best thing to do is get still and stop.

What's one particular cue that comforts you and allows you to quiet your mind in stressful situations?

How does this help you?

What hinders you?

How are you getting in your own way?

_____

_____

_____

_____

_____

_____

_____

_____

_____

_____

_____

_____

_____

_____

_____

_____

_____

_____

_____

Chapter 4: Freedom

Ask yourself the following questions and answer them truthfully:

What is it that makes it worth it for you to even consider changing?

_____

_____

_____

_____

_____

If things worked out exactly the way you wanted, what would be different?

_____

_____

_____

_____

_____

What are the pluses and minuses of changing and not changing?

_____

_____

_____

_____

_____

If this change were easy, would you want to make it?

_____

_____

_____

_____

What makes it hard?

_____

_____

_____

_____

_____

_____

_____

_____

_____

_____

_____

_____

_____

_____

_____

How are you getting in your own way?

_____

_____

_____

_____

_____

_____

_____

_____

_____

_____

_____

_____

_____

_____

_____

_____

_____

_____

_____

_____

_____

Chapter 5: Here Comes the Rain Again

Choose a time to talk with a friend, your partner, your child, or a colleague. Your task is to listen, really listen, without interrupting the other person. As Frank Ostaseski says, learn to listen and communicate from three levels—body, heart, and mind. Write down afterwards how you felt.

_____

_____

_____

_____

_____

_____

Write down how the other person felt.

_____

_____

_____

_____

_____

_____

_____

_____

_____

_____

_____

How are you getting in your own way?

_____

_____

_____

_____

_____

_____

_____

_____

_____

_____

_____

_____

_____

_____

_____

_____

_____

_____

_____

Chapter 6: Into the Groove

Note and record an IRIS moment or event that you have had.

What was your intention? What did you become aware of?

_____

_____

_____

_____

_____

_____

_____

_____

How are you getting in your own way?

_____

_____

_____

_____

_____

_____

_____

_____

_____

_____

Chapter 7: What Difference Does It Make?

Make notes, or use this when you have given feedback or wish to give feedback.

See it. You observe something that you do not understand or recognize as suitable behaviour.

Say it. Always with kind intention and with the aim to comprehend, ask open-ended questions.

Sort it. Together, work towards a mutual understanding, a constructive dialogue.

Post-reflection. What worked? What didn't work?

_____

_____

_____

_____

_____

_____

_____

_____

_____

_____

_____

How are you getting in your own way?

_____

_____

_____

_____

_____

_____

_____

_____

_____

_____

_____

_____

_____

_____

_____

_____

_____

_____

_____

_____

_____

_____

_____

Chapter 8: Non, Je ne Regrette Rien

Preparation before the dialogue—make notes on the following:

- What can you do to better understand differences/strengths?
- How can you leverage the communication?
- What are the obstacles for you and for the other?

_____

_____

_____

_____

_____

_____

_____

_____

_____

_____

_____

_____

_____

_____

_____

_____

_____

_____

How are you getting in your own way?

_____

_____

_____

_____

_____

_____

_____

_____

_____

_____

_____

_____

_____

_____

_____

_____

_____

_____

_____

Chapter 9: (Just Like) Starting Over

The one who sets the frame governs the experience. Before a difficult conversation, consider what you will say and in what way you will say it.

The next time you meet a person, remember that words have power, so choose yours wisely.

How can you reframe a setback as an opportunity?

_____

_____

_____

_____

_____

_____

How can you reframe a constraint as an advantage?

_____

_____

_____

_____

_____

_____

_____

_____

How are you getting in your own way?

_____

_____

_____

_____

_____

_____

_____

_____

_____

_____

_____

_____

_____

_____

_____

_____

_____

_____

Chapter 10: Stop to Love

Make notes on which areas need nourishment.

Emotional

_____

_____

_____

_____

_____

Spiritual

_____

_____

_____

_____

_____

Physical

_____

_____

_____

_____

_____

How are you getting in your own way?

_____

_____

_____

_____

_____

_____

_____

_____

_____

_____

_____

_____

_____

_____

_____

_____

_____

_____

_____

_____

_____

_____

Chapter 11: I Feel for You

What is the impact of your kindness on others?

_____

_____

_____

_____

_____

_____

What is the impact of your kindness on yourself?

_____

_____

_____

_____

_____

_____

How can your act of kindness create a ripple effect?

_____

_____

_____

_____

_____

How are you getting in your own way?

_____

_____

_____

_____

_____

_____

_____

_____

_____

_____

_____

_____

_____

_____

_____

_____

_____

_____

_____

_____

_____

Chapter 12: I'm Coming Out

What messages did you receive about women when you were growing up?

_____

_____

_____

_____

_____

What messages did you receive about women at school and later on?

_____

_____

_____

_____

_____

_____

How has that affected you today?

_____

_____

_____

_____

How are you getting in your own way?

_____

_____

_____

_____

_____

_____

_____

_____

_____

_____

_____

_____

_____

_____

_____

_____

_____

_____

_____

_____

_____

_____

Chapter 13: This Must Be the Place

What does it mean to you to be good enough?

_____

_____

_____

_____

_____

_____

When did you feel good enough?

_____

_____

_____

_____

_____

_____

Where were you? Who were you with?

_____

_____

_____

_____

_____

_____

How are you getting in your own way?

_____

_____

_____

_____

_____

_____

_____

_____

_____

_____

_____

_____

_____

_____

_____

_____

_____

_____

_____

Chapter 14: Gaata Rahe Mera Dil

_____

_____

_____

_____

_____

_____

_____

_____

_____

_____

Milestone moments:

_____

_____

_____

_____

_____

_____

_____

_____

_____

How can you stop getting in your own way?

Actions, strategies, and plans:

_____

_____

_____

_____

_____

_____

_____

_____

_____

_____

_____

_____

_____

_____

_____

_____

_____

_____

_____

Afterword: Loving-Kindness

> Life is under no obligation to give us what we expect. We
> take what we get and are thankful it is no worse than it is.
>
> Margaret Mitchell

Today take a moment to reflect on what you most want for yourself. Loving-kindness is a practice of wishing ourselves and others well. It is a humble approach to direct our attention away from judgements. This cultivates a sense of internal peace and empathy for ourselves and others. Cultivate this open-hearted, moment-to-moment, non-judgemental awareness.

In formal loving-kindness meditation practice, start by directing kind attention to yourself by silently saying to yourself every day the following things:

~ May I be happy.
~ May I be safe.
~ May I be healthy.
~ May I live with ease.

My hope for you is this:

May you be happy, may you be safe, may you be healthy, and may you live with ease.

Notes

With special thanks and gratitude

To Bernard Duboux and his wonderful sister, Danielle Duboux.

Some of the proceeds of this book will be donated to La Maison de Tara in recognition of all the unconditional love and care they provide to the residents, their families, the volunteers, and society.

.

Appendix A

This is the full text of Enoch Powell's so-called "Rivers of Blood" speech, which was delivered to a Conservative Association meeting in Birmingham on 20 April 1968.

The supreme function of statesmanship is to provide against preventable evils. In seeking to do so, it encounters obstacles which are deeply rooted in human nature.

One is that by the very order of things such evils are not demonstrable until they have occurred: at each stage in their onset there is room for doubt and for dispute whether they be real or imaginary. By the same token, they attract little attention in comparison with current troubles, which are both indisputable and pressing: whence the besetting temptation of all politics to concern itself with the immediate present at the expense of the future.

Above all, people are disposed to mistake predicting troubles for causing troubles and even for desiring troubles: *If only,* they love to think. *If only people wouldn't talk about it, it probably wouldn't happen.*

Perhaps this habit goes back to the primitive belief that the word and the thing, the name and the object, are identical.

At all events, the discussion of future grave but, with effort now, avoidable evils is the most unpopular and at the same time the most necessary occupation for the politician. Those who knowingly shirk it deserve, and not infrequently receive, the curses of those who come after.

A week or two ago I fell into conversation with a constituent, a middle-aged, quite ordinary working man employed in one of our nationalised industries.

After a sentence or two about the weather, he suddenly said: "If I had the money to go, I wouldn't stay in this country." I made some deprecatory reply to the effect that even this government wouldn't last for ever; but he took no notice, and continued: "I have three children, all of them been through grammar school and two of them married now, with family. I shan't be satisfied till I have seen them all settled overseas. In this country in 15 or 20 years' time the black man will have the whip hand over the white man."

I can already hear the chorus of execration. How dare I say such a horrible thing? How dare I stir up trouble and inflame feelings by repeating such a conversation?

The answer is that I do not have the right not to do so. Here is a decent, ordinary fellow Englishman, who in broad daylight in my own town says to me, his Member of Parliament, that his country will not be worth living in for his children.

I simply do not have the right to shrug my shoulders and think about something else. What he is saying, thousands and hundreds of thousands are saying and thinking—not throughout Great Britain, perhaps, but in the areas that are already undergoing the total transformation to which there is no parallel in a thousand years of English history.

In 15 or 20 years, on present trends, there will be in this country three and a half million Commonwealth immigrants and their descendants. That is not my figure. That is the official figure given to parliament by the spokesman of the Registrar General's Office.

There is no comparable official figure for the year 2000, but it must be in the region of five to seven million, approximately one-tenth of the whole population, and approaching that of Greater London. Of course, it will not be evenly distributed from Margate to Aberystwyth and from Penzance to Aberdeen. Whole areas, towns and parts of towns across England will be occupied by sections of the immigrant and immigrant-descended population.

As time goes on, the proportion of this total who are immigrant descendants, those born in England, who arrived here by exactly the same route as the rest of us, will rapidly increase. Already by 1985 the native-born would constitute the majority. It is this fact which creates the extreme urgency of action now, of just that kind of action which is hardest for politicians to take, action where the difficulties lie in the present but the evils to be prevented or minimised lie several parliaments ahead.

The natural and rational first question with a nation confronted by such a prospect is to ask: "How can its dimensions be reduced?" Granted it be not wholly preventable, can it be limited, bearing in mind that numbers are of the essence: the significance and consequences of an alien element introduced into a country or population are profoundly different according to whether that element is 1 per cent or 10 per cent.

The answers to the simple and rational question are equally simple and rational: by stopping, or virtually stopping, further inflow, and by promoting the maximum outflow. Both answers are part of the official policy of the Conservative Party.

It almost passes belief that at this moment 20 or 30 additional immigrant children are arriving from overseas in Wolverhampton alone every week—and that means 15 or 20 additional families a decade or two hence. Those whom the gods wish to destroy, they first make mad. We must be mad, literally mad, as a nation to be permitting the annual inflow of some 50,000 dependants, who are for the most part the material of the future growth of the immigrant-descended population. It is like watching a nation busily engaged in heaping up its own funeral pyre. So insane are we that we actually permit unmarried persons to immigrate for the purpose of founding a family with spouses and fiancés whom they have never seen.

Let no one suppose that the flow of dependants will automatically tail off. On the contrary, even at the present admission rate of only 5,000 a year by voucher, there is sufficient for a further 25,000 dependants per annum ad infinitum, without considering the huge reservoir of existing relations in this country—and I am making no allowance at all for fraudulent entry. In these circumstances nothing will suffice but that the total inflow for settlement should be reduced at once to negligible proportions, and that the necessary legislative and administrative measures be taken without delay.

I stress the words *for settlement*. This has nothing to do with the entry of Commonwealth citizens, any more than of aliens, into this country, for the purposes of study or of improving their qualifications, like (for instance) the Commonwealth doctors who, to the advantage of their own countries, have enabled our hospital service to be expanded faster than would otherwise have been possible. They are not, and never have been, immigrants.

I turn to re-emigration. If all immigration ended tomorrow, the rate of growth of the immigrant and immigrant-descended population would be substantially reduced, but the prospective size of this element in the population would still leave the basic character of the national danger unaffected. This can only be tackled while a considerable proportion of the total still comprises persons who entered this country during the last ten years or so.

Hence the urgency of implementing now the second element of the Conservative Party's policy: the encouragement of re-emigration.

Nobody can make an estimate of the numbers which, with generous assistance, would choose either to return to their countries of origin or to go to other countries anxious to receive the manpower and the skills they represent.

Nobody knows, because no such policy has yet been attempted. I can only say that, even at present, immigrants in my own constituency from time to time come to me, asking if I can find them assistance to return home. If such a policy were adopted and pursued with the determination which the gravity of the alternative justifies, the resultant outflow could appreciably alter the prospects.

The third element of the Conservative Party's policy is that all who are in this country as citizens should be equal before the law and that there shall be no discrimination or difference made between them by public authority. As Mr Heath has put it we will have no "first-class citizens" and "second-class citizens". This does not mean that the immigrant and his descendent should be elevated into a privileged or special class or that the citizen should be denied his right to discriminate in the management of his own affairs between one fellow citizen and another or that he should be subjected to imposition as to his reasons and motive for behaving in one lawful manner rather than another.

There could be no grosser misconception of the realities than is entertained by those who vociferously demand legislation as they call it "against discrimination", whether they be leader-writers of the same kidney and sometimes on the same newspapers which year after year in the 1930s tried to blind this country to the rising peril which confronted it, or archbishops who live in palaces, faring delicately with the bedclothes pulled right up over their heads. They have got it exactly and diametrically wrong.

The discrimination and the deprivation, the sense of alarm and of resentment, lies not with the immigrant population but with those among whom they have come and are still coming.

This is why to enact legislation of the kind before parliament at this moment is to risk throwing a match on to gunpowder. The kindest thing that can be said about those who propose and support it is that they know not what they do.

Nothing is more misleading than comparison between the Commonwealth immigrant in Britain and the American Negro. The Negro population of the United States, which was already in existence before the United States became a nation, started literally as slaves and were later given the franchise and other rights of citizenship, to the exercise of which they have only gradually and still incompletely come. The Commonwealth immigrant came to Britain as a full citizen, to a country which knew no discrimination between one citizen and another, and he entered instantly into the possession of the rights of every citizen, from the vote to free treatment under the National Health Service.

Whatever drawbacks attended the immigrants arose not from the law or from public policy or from administration, but from those personal circumstances and accidents which cause, and always will cause, the fortunes and experience of one man to be different from another's.

But while, to the immigrant, entry to this country was admission to privileges and opportunities eagerly sought, the impact upon the existing population was very different. For reasons which they could not comprehend, and in pursuance of a decision by default, on which they were never consulted, they found themselves made strangers in their own country.

They found their wives unable to obtain hospital beds in childbirth, their children unable to obtain school places, their homes and neighbourhoods changed beyond recognition, their plans and prospects for the future defeated; at work they found that employers hesitated to apply to the immigrant worker the standards of discipline and competence required of the native-born worker; they began to hear, as time went by, more and more voices which told them that they were now the unwanted. They now learn that a one-way privilege is to be established by act of parliament; a law which cannot, and is not intended to, operate to protect them or redress their grievances is to be enacted to give the stranger, the disgruntled and the agent-provocateur the power to pillory them for their private actions.

In the hundreds upon hundreds of letters I received when I last spoke on this subject two or three months ago, there was one striking feature which was largely new and which I find ominous. All Members of Parliament are used to the typical anonymous correspondent; but what surprised and alarmed me was the high proportion of ordinary, decent, sensible people, writing a rational and often well-educated letter, who believed that they had to omit their address because it was dangerous to have committed themselves to paper to a Member of Parliament agreeing with the views I had expressed, and that they would risk penalties or reprisals if they were known to have done so. The sense of being a persecuted minority which is growing among ordinary English people in the areas of the country which are affected is something that those without direct experience can hardly imagine.

I am going to allow just one of those hundreds of people to speak for me:

"Eight years ago, in a respectable street in Wolverhampton a house was sold to a Negro. Now only one white (a woman old-age pensioner) lives there. This is her story. She lost her husband and both her sons in the war. So, she turned her seven-roomed house, her only asset, into a boarding house. She worked hard and did well, paid off her mortgage and began to put something by for her old age. Then the immigrants moved in. With growing fear, she saw one house after another taken over. The quiet street became a place of noise and confusion. Regretfully, her white tenants moved out.

"The day after the last one left, she was awakened at 7 a.m. by two Negroes who wanted to use her 'phone to contact their employer. When she refused, as she would have refused any stranger at such an hour, she was abused and feared she would have been attacked but for the chain on her door. Immigrant families have tried to rent rooms in her house, but she always refused. Her little store of money went, and after paying rates, she has less than £2 per week.

"She went to apply for a rate reduction and was seen by a young girl, who on hearing she had a seven-roomed house, suggested she should let part of it. When she said the only people, she could get were Negroes, the girl said, 'Racial prejudice won't get you anywhere in this country.' So, she went home.

"The telephone is her lifeline. Her family pay the bill and help her out as best they can. Immigrants have offered to buy her house—at a price which the prospective landlord would be able to recover from his tenants in weeks, or at most a few months. She is becoming afraid to go out. Windows are broken. She finds excreta pushed through her letter box. When she goes to the shops, she is followed by children, charming, wide-grinning piccaninnies. They cannot speak English, but one word they know. 'Racialist,' they chant. When the new Race Relations Bill is passed, this woman is convinced she will go to prison. And is she so wrong? I begin to wonder."

The other dangerous delusion from which those who are wilfully or otherwise blind to realities suffer, is summed up in the word *integration*. To be integrated into a population means to become for all practical purposes indistinguishable from its other members.

Now, at all times, where there are marked physical differences, especially of colour, integration is difficult though, over a period, not impossible. There are among the Commonwealth immigrants who have come to live here in the last fifteen years or so, many thousands whose wish and purpose is to be integrated and whose every thought and endeavour is bent in that direction.

But to imagine that such a thing enters the heads of a great and growing majority of immigrants and their descendants is a ludicrous misconception, and a dangerous one.

We are on the verge here of a change. Hitherto it has been force of circumstance and of background which has rendered the very idea of integration inaccessible to the greater part of the immigrant population—that they never conceived or intended such a thing, and that their numbers and physical concentration meant the pressures towards integration which normally bear upon any small minority did not operate.

Now we are seeing the growth of positive forces acting against integration, of vested interests in the preservation and sharpening of racial and religious differences, with a view to the exercise of actual domination, first over fellow-immigrants and then over the rest of the population. The cloud no bigger than a man's hand, that can so rapidly overcast the sky, has been visible recently in Wolverhampton and has shown signs of spreading quickly. The words I am about to use, verbatim as they appeared in the local press on 17 February, are not mine, but those of a Labour Member of Parliament who is a minister in the present government:

"The Sikh communities' campaign to maintain customs inappropriate in Britain is much to be regretted. Working in Britain, particularly in the public services, they should be prepared to accept the terms and conditions of their employment. To claim special communal rights (or should one say rites?) leads to a dangerous fragmentation within society. This communalism is a canker; whether practised by one colour or another it is to be strongly condemned."

All credit to John Stonehouse for having had the insight to perceive that, and the courage to say it.

For these dangerous and divisive elements, the legislation proposed in the Race Relations Bill is the very pabulum they need to flourish. Here is the means of showing that the immigrant communities can organise to consolidate their members, to agitate and campaign against their fellow citizens, and to overawe and dominate the rest with the legal weapons which the ignorant and the ill-informed have provided. As I look ahead, I am filled with foreboding; like the Roman, I seem to see "the River Tiber foaming with much blood".

That tragic and intractable phenomenon which we watch with horror on the other side of the Atlantic but which there is interwoven with the history and existence of the States itself, is coming upon us here by our own volition and our own neglect. Indeed, it has all but come. In numerical terms, it will be of American proportions long before the end of the century.

Only resolute and urgent action will avert it even now. Whether there will be the public will to demand and obtain that action, I do not know. All I know is that to see, and not to speak, would be the great betrayal.

Appendix B

Gayatri Mantra, A Universal Prayer: Meaning and Significance

Reference: Sathya Sai International Organization

Om Bhur Bhuvaḥ Swaḥh
Tat-savitur Vareñyaṃ
Bhargo Devasya Dhīmahi
Dhiyo Yonaḥ Prachodayāt

General meaning: We meditate on that most adored Supreme Lord, the Creator, whose effulgence (divine light) illuminates all realms (physical, mental, and spiritual). May this divine light illuminate our intellect.

Word meanings:

- Om: the primeval sound
- Bhur: the physical body/physical realm
- Bhuvah: the life force/the mental realm
- Suvah: the soul/spiritual realm
- Tat: That (God)
- Savitur: the Sun, Creator (source of all life)
- Vareñyam: adore
- Bhargo: effulgence (divine light)

- Devasya: Supreme Lord
- Dhīmahi: meditate
- Dhiyo: the intellect
- Yo: May this light
- Prachodayāt: illumine/inspire

Aarti Shri Santoshi Maa Reference

Aarti is a Hindu ritual that is performed and sung to develop the highest love for God. In Sanskrit, *aa* means "towards", and *rati* means "the highest love for God". Aarti is a ceremony of worship that takes place in front of the deities. The priest has a tray with a small lighted oil diva lamp, burning incense, a small bell, offerings of food, a bowl of water, and flowers. The four elements—fire, earth, water, and air—are all represented.

Jai Santoshi Mata, Maiya Jai Santoshi Mata
Apane Sewak Jana Ko, Sukha Sampatti Data
Jai Santoshi Mata

Sundar Cheer Sunahari Maa Dharan Kinho
Heera Panna Damake, Tana Shringara Kinho
Jai Santoshi Mata

Geru Laala Chhata Chhavi, Badana Kamal Sohe
Manda Hansata Karunamayi, Tribhuvana Man Mohe
Jai Santoshi Mata

Swarna Sinhasana Baithi, Chanvar Dhure Pyare
Dhoop Deep Madhumeva, Bhoga Dhare Nyare
Jai Santoshi Mata

Gud Aru Chana Paramapriya, Tame Santosh Kiyo
Santoshi Kahalai, Bhaktana Vaibhav Diyo
Jai Santoshi Mata

Shukrawar Priya Manat, Aaja Diwas Sohi
Bhakta Mandali Chhai, Katha Sunat Mohi
Jai Santoshi Mata

Mandir Jagamaga Jyoti, Mangal Dhwani Chhai
Vinaya Kare Hama Balaka, Charanan Sira Nai
Jai Santoshi Mata

Bhakti Bhavamaya Puja, Angikrita Kijai□
Jo Man Basai Hamare, Ichchha Phala Dijai
Jai Santoshi Mata

Dukhi Daridri, Roga, Sankat Mukta Kiye
Bahu Dhana-Dhanya Bhare Ghara, Sukha Saubhagya Diye
Jai Santoshi Mata

Dhyana Dharyo Jisa Jana Ne, Manavanchhita Phala Payo
Puja Katha Shrawan Kar, Ghara Ananda Ayo
Jai Santoshi Mata

Sharan Gahe Ki Lajja, Rakhiyo Jagadambe
Sankat Tu Hi Niware, Dayamayi Ambe
Jai Santoshi Mata

Santoshi Maa Ki Aarti, Jo Koi Jana Gave
Riddhi-Siddhi, Sukha-Sampatti, Ji Bharakara Pave
Jai Santoshi Mata

BIBLIOGRAPHY

Angelou, Maya, "Still I Rise", in *And Still I Rise: A Book of Poems* (New York: Random House, 1978).

Auerbach, E. A. "Cognitive Coaching", in D. Stober and A. M. Grant, eds, *Evidence-Based Coaching Handbook* (New York, 2006).

Be Mindful, http://bemindful.co.uk/.

Berg, I. K., and Szabo, P., *Brief Coaching for Lasting Solutions* (New York, 2005).

Coleman, Cassie, *Hinduism—Adopting Hinduism as a Way of Life: Hinduism for Beginners, Beliefs and Practices* (2016).

Connor, Mary, and Pokora, Julia, *Coaching and Mentoring at Work* (Sales Handle, 2012).

Cuddy, Amy, "Your Body Language May Shape Who You Are" [video], TEDGlobal 2012 (June 2012), https://www.ted.com/talks/amy_cuddy_your_body_language_shapes_who_you_are?language=en, accessed 21 Feb. 2019.

Delizonna, Laura, "High-Performing Teams Need Psychological Safety. Here's How to Create It", 24 Aug. 2017, https://hbr.org/2017/08/high-performing-teams-need-psychological-safety-heres-how-to-create-it.

Duhigg, Charles, "What Google Learned from Its Quest to Build the Perfect Team", 25 Feb. 2016, https://www.nytimes.com/2016/02/28/magazine/what-google-learned-from-its-quest-to-build-the-perfect-team.html?smid=pl-share.

Ericsson, Anders, and Pool, Robert, *Peak: Secrets from the New Science of Expertise* (2016).

Freedman, J., and Everett, T., *A Business Case for Emotional Intelligence* (2nd edn, 2008).

"The Frustrations of Non-Directive Coaching", *People Management*, http://www.peoplemanagement.co.uk/pm/blog-posts/2010/03/the-frustrations-of-non-directive-coaching.htm.

Gallwey, W. Timothy, *The Inner Game of Tennis: The Classic Guide to the Mental Side of Peak Performance* (1997).

Goldsmith, Marshall, *What Got You Here Won't Get You There: How Successful People Become Even More Successful* (2007).

Goleman, Daniel, *Emotional Intelligence: Why It Can Matter More than IQ* (New York: Bantam Books, 1995).

Goleman, Daniel, *Working with Emotional Intelligence* (New York: Bantam Books, 1998).

Grange Hill, British television children's drama series originally produced by the BBC. The show, created by Phil Redmond, began its run on 8 Feb. 1978, on BBC1.

Grant, A. M., and Stober, D., "Introduction", in *Evidence-Based Coaching Handbook* (New York: Wiley, 2006).

Harvard Business Review staff, "Breakthrough Ideas for Tomorrow's Business Agenda", *Organizational Culture Magazine* and *Harvard Business Review*, http://www.humancapitalreview.org/content/default.asp?Article_ID=8&ArticlePage_ID=16&cntPage=2, accessed 25 Nov. 2011.

Hewlett, Sylvia Ann, *Executive Presence: The Missing Link between Merit and Success* (Harper Business, 3 June 2014).

Institute of Leadership Management, "Creating a Coaching Culture", research report, http://www.i-l-m.com/research-and-comment/9617.aspx.

International Journal of Evidence-Based Coaching and Mentoring, 6/2 (August 2008), 113.

Lieberman, M. D., "Social Cognitive Neuroscience: A Review of Core Processes", *The Annual Review of Psychology*, 58 (2007), 259–89.

Lieberman, M. D., Eisenberger, N. I., Crockett, M. J., Tom, S. M., Pfeifer, J. H., and B. M. Way, "Putting Feelings into Words", *Psychological Science*, 18/5 (June 2007), 421–8.

Miller, Ali, "Loving Kindness Mediation: Befriending Ourselves", http://www.befriendingourselves.com/Lovingkindness.html.

Mind Tools, http://www.mindtools.com/index.html.

Nadler, R. S., *Leadership Keys Field Guide: Emotional Intelligence Tools for Great Leadership* (Santa Barbara: Psyccess Press, 2007).

"Name That Feeling: You'll Feel Better", *Scientific American* (June 2007).

Neenan, M., and Dryden, W., *Life Coaching: A Cognitive-Behavioural Approach* (2002).

"New National Rail Security Campaign Starts Today: 'See It. Say It. Sorted.'" The nationwide campaign to encourage train passengers and station visitors to report any unusual items or activity was launched on Tuesday, 1 Nov. 2016, by Rail Minister Paul Maynard at London's Waterloo station.

O'Broin, Alanna, and Palmer, Stephen, *Co-creating an Optimal Coaching Alliance: A Cognitive Behavioral Coaching Perspective* (2008).

The Oprah Winfrey Show (25 May 2011).

Ostaseski, Frank, and Remen, Rachel Naomi, *The Five Invitations: Discovering What Death Can Teach Us about Living Fully* (Deckle Edge, 14 Mar. 2017).

Rogers, C. R., *Client-Centered Therapy: Its Current Practice, Implications, and Theory* (Boston: Houghton Mifflin, 1951).

Sathya, Sai, "International Organisation", http://www.sathyasai.org/.

Schein, Edgar H., *Helping: How to Offer, Give, and Receive Help* (2011).

Sehmi, Sunita, "How to Reach Your Peak—an Interview with Anders Ericsson" (19 Jan. 2018), https://www.knowitall.ch/

blogs/work-business/sunita-sehmi/2236-how-to-reach-your-peak-an-interview-with-anders-ericsson.

Sehmi, Sunita, "An interview with Andy Puddicombe, Meditation and Mindfulness Expert and Co-founder of Headspace", https://www.knowitall.ch/blogs/work-business/sunita-sehmi/1378-an-interview-with-andy-puddicombe-meditation-and-mindfulness-expert-and-co-founder-of-headspace.

Sehmi, Sunita, "Following Your Spouse Abroad: How to Reinvent Yourself", February 2012, https://www.internations.org/guide/global/following-your-spouse-abroad-reinvent-yourself-16659.

Taylor, Bill, "It's More important to Be Kind than Clever", *Harvard Business Review* (23 Aug. 2012), http://blogs.hbr.org/taylor/2012/08/its_more_important_to_be_kind.html, accessed 21 Feb. 2019.

Thaler, Linda Kaplan, and Koval, Robin, "The Power of Nice: How to Conquer the Business World with Kindness".

Tolle, Eckhart, *The Power of Now: A Guide to Spiritual Enlightenment Paperback* (2004).

Ware, Bronnie, *The Top Five Regrets of the Dying: A Life Transformed by the Dearly Departing* (20 Mar. 2012).

Whitmore, J., *Coaching for Performance* (London: Nicholas Brealey Publishing, 2003).

Whitmore, John, *Coaching for Performance: GROWing Human Potential and Purpose—The Principles and Practice of Coaching and Leadership* (4th edn, 2009).

Zukav, Gary, *The Seat of the Soul* (1990).

Song Reference List

Cole, Lloyd, and the Commotions, "Forest Fire", in *Rattlesnakes*, Al Dubin and Harry Warren, released 12 October 1984.

Costello, Elvis, and the Attractions, "Every Day I Write the Book", in *Punch the Clock*, prod. Clive Langer and Alan Winstanley, assisted by Gavin Greenaway and Colin Fairley, released 1983 (F-Beat).

Eurythmics, "Here Comes the Rain Again", Annie Lennox and David A. Stewart, prod. David A. Stewart, released 12 January 1984.

Houston, Whitney, "I'm Every Woman", in *The Bodyguard*, Nickolas Ashford and Valerie Simpson, prod. Narada, Michael Walden, Louis Biancaniello, David Cole, and Robert Clivillés, released 2 January 1993 (Arista).

Khan, Chaka, "I Feel for You", in *I Feel for You*, prod. Arif Mardin and David Foster, released 1 October 1984 (Warner Bros.).

Kumar, Kishore, and Mangeshkar, Lata, "Gaata Rahe Mera Dil", in *Guide*, sung by Sachin Dev Burman, prod. Sachin Dev Burman, released 1965 (India).

Lennon, John, "(Just Like) Starting Over", in *Double Fantasy*, John Lennon, prod. John Lennon, Yoko Ono, and Jack Douglas, released 24 October 1980 (Geffen).

Madonna, "Into the Groove", in *Like a Virgin*, Madonna and Stephen Bray, prod. Madonna and Stephen Bray, released 23 July 1985.

Pet Shop Boys with Dusty Springfield, "What Have I Done to Deserve This?" in *Actually*, released 10 August 1987.

Piaf, Édith, "Non, je ne regrette rien", Michel Vaccaire, comp. Charles Dumont, released 1960.

Ross, Diana, "I'm Coming Out", in *Diana*, prod. Bernard Edwards and Nile Rodgers, released 22 August 1980.

The Smiths, "What Difference Does It Make?" in *The Smiths*, Johnny Marr and Morrissey, prod. John Porter, released 16 January 1984 (Rough Trade).

Springsteen, Bruce, "Dancing in the Dark", in *Born in the USA*, prod. Steven Van Zandt, Bruce Springsteen, Chuck Plotkin, and Jon Landau, released 1984.

Talking Heads, "This Must Be the Place (Naive Melody)", in *Speaking in Tongues*, David Byrne, Chris Frantz, Jerry Harrison, and Tina Weymouth, prod. Talking Heads, released November 1983 (Sire).

Vandross, Luther, "Stop to Love Single", in *Give Me the Reason*, Luther Vandross and Marcus Miller, released August 1986 (Epic).

Wham, "Freedom", George Michael, prod. George Michael, released 13 August 1984.

About the Author

Sunita is an executive coach, consultant, and facilitator. She is the founder of Walk the Talk, a consultancy firm with the objective of getting people to realise their true potential and helping leaders and their teams to create more safety, inclusion, and belonging. She provides advice to companies and NGOs worldwide. Her clients include the GAVI Alliance, Facebook, IMD Business School, the Tata Group, McKinsey, Novartis, and CERN, to name a few. Her overriding mission is to help people get out of their own way.

Sunita brings over 25 years' experience and knowledge. She has a rich and diverse background; she is Indian, British, and Swiss, which allows her to deeply connect with and understand her clients whatever their background and wherever they are operating in the world. Indeed, she is an inclusion champion.

Sunita studied organisational psychology and development of adults at the bachelor's level. She holds a master's degree in coaching and career management from the University of Geneva. She is an ICF executive coach and an NLP practitioner and is certified by the INSEAD Gender Diversity Programme.

In her free time, Sunita is a pro bono mentor for the Richard Branson Centre of Entrepreneurship and the Cherie Blair Foundation for Women and is a volunteer at the hospice La Maison de Tara. An avid writer, Sunita is a contributor to Thrive Global.

She lives in Geneva with her husband and her two boys.

Acknowledgements

I would like to thank all the people who have come into my life. Some have stayed, and some have left. They have all taught me great lessons and have enabled me to be the person I am today. I would also like to thank Switzerland. I owe this land of chocolate and cheese so much. You gave me the freedom to be myself, you gave me emancipation, and you gave me my beautiful three musketeers, and for that I am eternally grateful.

Lightning Source UK Ltd.
Milton Keynes UK
UKHW020616100719
345903UK00005B/103/P